Cricut

Beginners

The Ultimate Guide to Cricut Maker, Cricut Explore Air 2, and Cricut Design Space, Tips and Tricks to Start Making Real your Cricut Projects Ideas Today!

ROSE PAPER

Table of Content

Chapter 1: What Is a Cricut Machine and How Does It Work?

What Is a Cricut Machine?

A Cricut machine (also known as a craft plotter or die-cutting machine) is a personal cutting machine. It is similar to a desktop printer; images and designs printed on a computer are sent to the machine. Except that instead of printing the design, the machine moves a blade around to cut out the desired material.

The Cricut machine works automatically and can cut through materials such as paper, vinyl, craft foam, fabric, metal, faux leather, sticker paper, and even adhesive sheets.

There are models of the machine that allow users to use a pen rather than cutting to write texts and draw images, and can be used to produce wedding and party invitations that look handwritten.

The designs are digitally stored, thus, users can select and edit different patterns on their personal computers or mobile devices. Furthermore, there is a Cricut Image Library with over 50,000 images, fonts, and projects that users can choose from.

How Does the Cricut Machine Work?

First of all, Cricut machines are electrical appliances and as such, require power to work. Similar to the workings of the ink nozzle in a printer, they have a tiny computer located within the machine that controls a cutting blade. They use digital cutters that can be connected to a computer through Bluetooth and wireless.

What Can I Make with a Cricut Machine?

There is a lot that can be done with a Cricut machine. The possibilities are limitless, the following are a few examples:

- Make custom bags, shirts, or hats using iron-on (heat transfer) vinyl.

- Cut quilt square and appliqués.

- Create and produce customs cards for events like holiday cards, party invitations, and thank you notes, etc.

- Make window clings using static cling vinyl.

- Make and address envelopes.

- Print and cut out stickers.

- Etch glass.

- Make stencils for etching and spray painting.

- Create Christmas ornaments.

- Produce wall decals.

- Produce vinyl decals for shot glasses, mugs, champagne glasses, etc.

- Make leather bracelets.

- Cut out letters and shapes for scrapbooking.

- Make monogram pillows.

- Make painted wooden signs.

- Make window clings.

- Label items in a playroom or pantry.

Chapter 2: Cricut Explore Air 2 vs. Cricut Maker

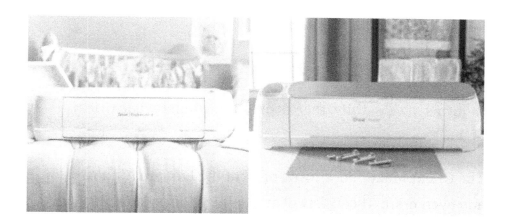

When the Cricut Maker was introduced to the public in the summer of 2017, one of the buzzing questions was; how does it compare to the Cricut Explore Air 2?

It's a valid question because the Cricut Explore 2 (a fantastic machine) had just been released as well, and is, by all standards, a fantastic cutting machine.

The truth is that both are excellent stand-alone machines that are extremely efficient at what they are designed for; however, there are pros and cons associated with both, and each crafter will be more suited to either one.

The fight between the Cricut Maker and the Explore Air 2 is on, and this is an opportunity for you to examine the right choice of cutter for you closely.

Below are some comparisons:

i. Versatility

In terms of versatility, there's only one winner—The Cricut Maker!

The Cricut Maker does 100% of what the Explore Air 2 can do and even more. It consists of an adaptive tool system that can cut over 100 different materials and a huge library of sewing patterns. When you consider all this, you'll realize that the Cricut Maker is versatile enough to work with a variety of tools—including all types of blades released by Cricut, the brand new knife, rotary blades, and the yet to be released ones as well.

You don't have to look any further because the rotary blade that comes with the Cricut Maker during purchase already puts it above the Explore Air 2.

The blade needs no supporting or backing material because it easily cuts through all types of fabric.

In theory, the Explore Air 2 is capable of cutting fabric, but not as good as the Maker. Thus, a backing material is always required because the fine blade often catches on the fabric.

Furthermore, users of the Explore Air 2 machine always use separate fabric cutters to get their desired cuts, but in contrast, the Maker is an all-purpose machine that does it all.

ii. Cutting Specs

When we talk about cutting specs, we are referring to the machine that cuts best. Besides, cutting is the reason why people even go out to buy the machine in the first place.

If you consider the price (entry-level price) of the Cricut Explore Air 2, you'll agree with me that it is extremely cost-effective. The machine remains one of the best cutters around because its German-made carbide blade cuts through materials with extreme ease, and that's why it is used to make designs that are small and intricate.

In contrast, the Cricut Maker comes with blades that aren't only sharp and precise, but also possess a lot more force behind them, it has about 4,000 grams of force, whereas the Explore Air comes with a paltry 400 grams only.

The Cricut Maker cuts easier and neater, requires fewer passes on thicker materials, and can work with way more materials than the Explore Air. Furthermore, the Marker is designed to potentially work with newer and sophisticated blades (such as the knife blade and rotary blade), as opposed to the Explore Air.

In terms of fabric cutting, the rotary blade remains a revolutionary invention that has greatly improved the industry, however, the knife blade has proven to be safer and more effective—it is the ultimate tool for cutting thick materials.

The Explore Air 2 is a highly efficient cutting machine that is perfectly suited for crafters that stick to thin materials, and do not require any special intervention.

The maximum cutting size of both machines is 12" wide by 24" long, and most industry experts are of the view that the Maker's cut size should have been increased to at least the size of the Silhouette Cameo 3 (12" wide by 10' long).

iii. Price

It is obvious that the Cricut Maker is an improved version of the Explore Air 2; however, many people agree that those improved features fail to justify the hike in price.

The Cricut Maker is listed at $399.99 on the Cricut website, and although it comes with improved features, many people see it as a significant amount to lay down on a cutter.

On the other hand, the Explore Air 2 is listed at $299.99 and during sales, the price drops down significantly.

iv. Longevity

Generally, when people weigh their options for products they intend to purchase, most times, they consider price ahead of other factors, but the truth is that price isn't everything. Thus, another factor to look out for is the products' longevity.

In terms of longevity, the Cricut Maker and the Explore Air 2 are very solid machines and there's absolutely no doubt about their durability. However, the Maker seems to be more suited for the future because the cutter will ultimately outlive more than the Explore Air 2.

Besides, the Cricut Maker comes with the Adaptive Tool System, meaning that it is guaranteed that it'll be compatible with all types of blades and tools that will be released in the foreseeable future.

No matter how much the crafting process evolves over the next couple of years, the Cricut Maker will remain effective and relevant.

On the other hand, the Explore Air 2 is not designed to offer more than it already does, and although it won't become obsolete, it just can't support the newer blades and tools that are being released by Cricut.

In comparison, the Explore Air 2 is meant for people that are happy with their available options and are concerned about upgrading their skills, whereas the Cricut Maker is suitable for people that intend to experiment and develop their crafts further.

v. Software

In terms of software, there's nothing that separates these two machines because they both use the Cricut Design Space software.

Design Space Software is a decent program that is easy to use and contains plenty of editing options for users to effectively personalize their designs.

Users can upload their designs and convert them free of charge; thus, expert users can create their complex designs in more sophisticated programs like Adobe Illustrator, Corel Draw, Make the Cut, and Sure Cuts A Lot.

Cricut Design Space is cloud-based, so users can design on their personal computers, tablets, and phones.

It is a user-friendly program, but it has its flaws: sometimes, it gets buggy and limiting, especially while creating new designs within the program.

vi. Sewing Projects

In terms of the usage for sewing projects, it's not a contest! The Explore Air 2 is a versatile machine, but it doesn't measure up to the Cricut Maker.

On the other hand, apart from the actual sewing machine, the Cricut Maker is what people use for serious sewing projects. The Maker comes with a library that contains plenty of sewing patterns, and it not only cuts the patterns, it also marks them with the washable fabric marker pen. The Cricut Maker eliminates guesswork regarding the marking of patterns, which ultimately improves the final output of the work.

vii. Portability

One of the most important but often overlooked features of machines is portability. If you're a crafter that prefers to be static, then you can overlook it, but if you're someone who prefers to travel with your cutting machine, then you have to consider the size of the machine.

Between the two machines, the Cricut Maker is the heaviest, weighing almost 24 lbs. as against the Explore Air 2 that weighs only 14.8 lbs.

The Cricut Maker is a static machine specifically designed for use in a specialized space, home, or craft room. It has plenty of storage space and even comes with a provision for charging phones and/or tablets.

The Explore Air 2 is nimble and it comes with a smaller amount of storage; thus, it is perfect for people that like to craft on the road.

In terms of portability and ease of movement, the Explore Air 2 stands taller than the Cricut Maker.

viii. Ease of use

Both machines are relatively easy to use with little practice, but in terms of ease of use, the Cricut Maker edges the Explore Air 2.

The Explore Air 2 is built with the Smart Set Dial on the front and this allows users to easily select from the most common materials. Once the dial is set, the machine automatically adjusts its cut settings accordingly.

However, the problem most users face is that most of the materials the cutters use are not always the most common materials for members of the larger Cricut community. Thus, you have to manually set the material settings from within Design Space if your material isn't on the dial.

It is not an extremely difficult process, but it is a bit frustrating, especially when you have to carry out the same procedure over and over again.

On the other hand, the Cricut Maker automatically adjusts its settings according to the type of material that is loaded on the cutting mat.

It is extremely easy, and the user doesn't have to do any settings at all.

ix. Cartridges

Newcomers in the world of Cricut and the cutting of crafts might not understand this; however, long-time Cricut users will know all about the cartridges—they might even have a space dedicated to them in their craft rooms.

It is no longer mandatory to use cartridges for designs on both the Cricut Maker and the Explore Air 2.

However, in case you have a couple of old cartridges at home, you might want to use them; thus, you can plug them directly into the Explore Air 2, and use.

It is possible to use the cartridges with the Cricut Maker, but it is a bit more complex. You will have to get the cartridge adapter that will allow you to link the physical cartridges into Design

Space. The cartridge adapter uses a USB port to connect the Cartridges with the Maker.

There is also the option of using digital cartridges instead of buying the adapter. These are downloaded directly into Design Space.

x. Print Then Cut

The last and final battle between the Explorer Air 2 and the Cricut Maker is which of the machines have a better Print Then Cut.

The Cricut Maker comes with the Print Then Cut (PtC) feature, which allows users to print out their designs onto a white paper and then cut.

This feature comes in handy for crafters that tend to experiment more on new designs, as opposed to just downloading designs from Cricut Design Space.

The Explore Air 2 also has the same PtC feature as the Cricut Maker; however, the difference is that the Cricut Maker can PtC on colored and patterned paper, while the Explore Air 2 can't.

Thus, in terms of PtC, the Cricut Maker edges the Explore Air 2.

Overall Verdict

At this point, it is obvious that the Cricut Maker is the superior machine.

It is more durable, offers better Print Then Cut functionality, easier to use, more versatile, and an all-round better cutter.

The Explore Air 2 is a very good machine that has served crafters for some time now and will continue to do in the future; however, the Cricut Maker is just too good for it.

The Explore Air is the perfect machine for crafters that use paper, thin materials, cartridges, and also those that have a limited budget.

Both machines are highly efficient, and they serve their purposes perfectly; the Cricut Maker is for makers, while the Explore Air 2 is for cutting crafters.

Chapter 3: Insights of Explore Air 2 Machine: How to Design, Clean, Material That Can Be Used, Etc.

For you to be reading this, you are either thinking of acquiring a Cricut Explorer Air 2, or you already own one, and you're still trying to figure out how to use the machine efficiently.

Below is a breakdown of the Cricut Explore Air 2.

How to Make Your First Design

It is relatively easy to start designing with the Explore Air 2, and right now, you'll be shown a sample project that you can embark on with the materials that come with the machine during purchase.

Turn on your computer and go to design.cricut.com; on the page, click on the menu icon at the top left corner and click on New Machine Setup.

Note: Before you proceed, you need to have the following; sliver pen, cutting mat, paper, and sample cardstock. Also, you have to remove the protective film on the cutting mat and set it aside.

i.   Attach the grey cardstock on the cutting mat. Line it vertically on the mat, with the textured side facing up. It should be under the Cricut logo, at the top left corner.

ii.   Load the mat into the machine, follow the mat guides and insert the mat. Make sure you continuously press the mat firmly against the rollers while tapping the "load/unload" button at the top right of the machine (the icon is a set of double arrows).

iii. Install the silver pen, unlock the accessory clamp A. Remove the pen cap and position it to tip down into the housing until the arrow on the pen disappears. Close the clamp. **Note**: Remember to put the cap at the end of the pen when you're cutting, so that you won't lose it.

iv.   Look at the design on the mat preview screen. Hit "Go!"

v.   On the machine, set the dial to cardstock.

vi.   At this point, the "C" button should be flashing continuously. Hit the button to begin the design and watch the process.

vii.   Remove the mat; when the project is done, press the load/unload button and take off the pen.

viii.   You can keep it in the accessory compartment or the handy bin on the left-hand side of the machine.

ix.   On a clean surface, place the cutting map face down and fold the edge of it up toward you. At this point, the material will peel away from the mat; thus, you should continue pulling and folding the mat.

x.   Overlap the card over, fold it in half. Repeat the process with your blue paper and put it inside the grey card. If possible, you use glue to hold it together.

xi.   Finally, your first design is done!

What Are the Dos and Don'ts for Cleaning Your Cricut Explore Air?

So, you've made a wise investment because you bought the Cricut Explore Air 2 and you're in love with it. Now, you have to ensure that you're taking good care of the machine, right?

The Explore Air is a very efficient machine and with all the vinyl cutting, glitter paper cutting, cardstock cutting, and other materials that are used, it tends to get dirty from time to time. Thus, in order to keep your machine sparkling and new, these are the dos and don'ts:

Dos:

- Always ensure that you turn off the machine before cleaning

- Make sure to use a clean and soft cloth to wipe down the machine, e.g., nonalcoholic baby wipes

- Always clean the rollers in order to remove residue

- It is important to keep the blade housing clean at all times

- Thus, clean it whenever you use the machine in order to remove residue

- You can also shift the housing unit in order to clean the case properly

Don'ts:

- Do not clean the machine while it's on

- Do not directly spray cleaner on the machine

- You must not touch the gear chain at the rear of the machine

- Do not clean the bar that holds the housing because the grease is always meant to be there

How Do I Clean a Cricut Mat?

Cricut machines use sticky mats called Cricut mats and are supposed to be used for about 25–40 times, but if they are cleaned and maintained properly, they can last longer. Thus, in order to ensure a longer lifespan for the mat, you can either do light cleaning to maintain the stickiness or deeper cleaning when it has gotten extremely dirty. Even if you've used the mat to the extent that it loses its stickiness, you do certain things to add new layers of stickiness:

- When the mat loses some of its stickiness, give it some light cleaning; in order to make sure that your mat lasts for as long as possible, you should endeavor to clean it regularly. Use a plastic scraper to scrape it off, then roll a roller over the surface or wipe it with an alcohol-free baby wipe. **Note**: Baby wipes remove debris without destroying the mat because they wet down the surface gently. Also, lint rollers can remove debris from the mat because they are stickier than the mat.

- Use water and soap on the surface: When the mat begins to lose its stickiness after some time, you'll need to give it a light scrub. Pour warm water and soap on the surface and use a brush to scrub lightly. When you're done, rinse the surface with warm water. You can also use a Magic Eraser because it is good at removing residue and also gentle on the surface.

- Use a degreaser to spray the mat: This is recommended if the mat is extremely dirty and has completely lost its stickiness. Degreasers are capable of removing all sorts of debris on the mat but are also known to leave a residue too. Thus, after using the degreaser, you need to use soap and water to wash the mat. **Note**: A strong degreaser is capable of completely removing the mat's stickiness; however, you can get back the stickiness when the mat is clean and dry.

- Air-dry the mat: After washing the mat, you can either hang it or put it in a drying rack so that both sides can dry simultaneously. Also, irrespective of the type of cleaning you embark on, you must allow the mat to dry completely before you use it in the machine. **Note**: Wetness can greatly reduce the mat's stickiness and even potentially damage the machine. Do not try to dry the mat with a towel because it will cover the surface with fiber and minimize the mat's effectiveness.

How Do I Make a Cricut Mat Sticky Again?

i. Use a stickiness remover or alcohol to remove the original sticky layer: If you intend to get materials to stick to your mat, you should, first of all, take off the layer that has lost its stickiness. To achieve this, you can use a stickiness removing product like Goo Gone, or by rubbing alcohol on the surface. Also, in order to remove the old surface, you'll need the scraper that comes with the Cricut tools pack.

ii. Use tape to cover the edges of the mat: The part of the mat that is pulled through the machine's rollers are the edges, thus, they need to be free of stickiness. In order to make sure the edges don't get sticky, you can use masking tape or painter's tape to cover the edges. It is very simple because the affected edges are marked on the mat with color (the 4 colored edges are outside the grid pattern).

iii. Use a repositionable adhesive to cover the surface: In terms of the rejuvenation of Cricut mats, there are several adhesive products that are used. Most are readily available from online retailers and at craft stores. In terms of application, you can brush some on the surface, while some are sprayed. Some examples of adhesives that work are:

- Quilt basting spray

- Repositionable scrapbooking glue

- Repositionable spray adhesive

- Repositionable glue sticks

- Tacky glue thinned out with an equal part of water

iv. Allow the adhesive to dry completely: When you used the adhesive on the surface, it is important to allow it dry completely because it will ensure that the adhesive is properly bonded to the mat, thus, maintaining optimum stickiness. When the mat is completely dry, you can take off the tape and make use of the mat.

What Are the Materials Used for Cleaning the Cricut Mat?

- Alcohol-free baby wipe

- Plastic scraper

- Magic eraser

- Lint roller

- Degreaser

- Dish soap

What Are the Materials Used for Making a Mat Sticky Again?

- Plastic scraper

- Rubbing alcohol

- Masking tape or painter's tape

- Stickiness remover

- Repositionable adhesive

Warning:

You must be aware of the fact that the addition of stickiness to your Cricut mat voids all forms of warranty that comes with the Cricut machine. Generally, most machines come with a 1-year warranty from the date of purchase.

Chapter 4: Tools and Accessories Needed to Work with Explore Air 2 Machine

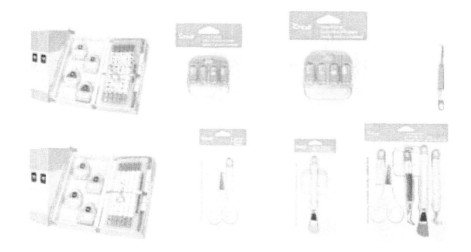

i. Cricut Basic Tools

- **Cricut Scraper:** Is used to remove and clean unwanted scraps from the cutting mat. It comes in handy when crafters do complex cuttings and have plenty of tiny pieces stuck to the mat. It can also be used to smooth out vinyl.

- **Micro-Tip Scissors**: Are used for cutting.

- **Weeder**: Is used in removing tiny cuts. It can be used for vinyl text.

- **Cricut Tweezers:** Are used to lift tiny and delicate pieces of materials.

- **Cricut Spatula**: Used to lift images from the mat. You can use it when you make delicate cuts, in order to avoid tearing the image.

ii. Cricut Cutting Mat

The latest Cricut cutting mats are designed with the weight of commonly used crafting materials in mind. Right now, there are three types of mats built to work with materials of different weights, including:

- One 12" x 12" Strong Grip Adhesive cutting mat

- One 12" x 12" Standard Grip Adhesive cutting mat

- One 12" x 12" Light Grip Adhesive cutting mat

At purchase, the machine comes with a standard grip mat (green); however, you have to understand that certain projects and materials require the use of different mats.

iii. Cricut Explore Pen Set

You can get the ultimate pen to customize a banner, write a greeting card, add heartfelt messages to your memories, and lots more.

The Cricut Explore Pen set includes:

The (one) 0.8 medium tip, (two) 0.3 tip, and (two) 0.8 medium calligraphy tip pens.

iv. Extras

- **Cricut Scoring Stylus**: The scoring stylus is used to ensure a neat fold line. It is installed in slot A of the explore machine.
- **Port Trimmer**: The trimmer is used for producing accurate and precise straight lines. I am of the habit of cutting the edges of my vinyl in order to line them up perfectly on my mat. The trimmer comes with a scoring blade and a substitute blade.

Chapter 5: Insights of Cricut Maker: How to Design, Clean, Material That Can Be Used, Etc.

In terms of appearance, the Cricut Maker is similar to the Explore line of machines, but the engineering in this one is totally different. It is a highly proficient machine and below are some of the features.

i. Design

The Cricut Maker has an unbelievable cutting pressure, and at the time it was released in 2017, it had more cutting pressure than most commercial cutting machines available. With the

Cricut Maker, crafters can easily cut thicker materials like chipboard and leather, as well as delicate materials like crepe paper and fabric, etc.

The Adaptive Tool System is another awesome feature of the Cricut Maker; it uses advanced mathematical algorithms and other complex gears to enhance cutting precision. With the Adaptive Tool System, new tools can always be introduced, e.g., the recently launched scoring wheel and knife blade.

Other features of the Maker include a docking station for mobile devices and a USB port for charging devices. The tool storage has been upgraded with a bigger storage bin and two tool cups (compared to the Explore machines).

The machine looks really good, and the materials are up to scratch, looking like an Apple product, with user experience and design topping the list of Cricut's priorities.

ii. Cricut Maker Machine Rotary Blade & Sewing Features

The rotary blade that comes with the Cricut Maker is a surprise because it was built with fabric in mind; Cricut literally solved the problems related to the cutting and marking of fabrics.

With the 12 mm rotary blade, crafters can cut straight fabric with the highest precision. Other notable features are the pink fabric mat and the washable fabric pen, which mark fabrics for crafters.

In terms of Design Space, Cricut has partnered with other brands such as Rile Blake and Simplicity to add some more digital sewing patterns. With the 12" x 24" mat, you can create large projects like a quilt, with smaller pieces. Finally, the Cricut Machine cuts your materials and marks them exactly the way you want.

iii. Cricut Maker Knife Blade

The knife blade was designed to cut thicker materials; it uses several passes to cut—starts with a lighter scoring line, then increases the force in the middle of the material, and ends with a lighter pass to get a very clean cut.

iv. Scoring Wheel

As an update to the scoring stylus, Cricut came out with the scoring wheel in 2018. This upgrade mostly affects paper crafters because it relieves all the woes related to scoring, e.g., it takes care of cracking materials and faint scores, etc.

v. Print Then Cut Upgrades

Unlike the Cricut Explore sensor that could only read registration marks on white paper, the Cricut Maker sensor can be used with colored and printed papers.

How to Design on Cricut Maker

Items needed:

- Inkspace or Adobe Illustrator software

- Cricut Design Studio software

- Cricut mat

- Computer

- Foam, paper, or vinyl

- Sure Cuts a Lot software

Step 1

Create your design using Inkspace or Adobe Illustrator. When you open the app, open a new file, and use the drawing tools available to make your own design.

Step 2

Press "file," "path," and then "trace bitmap." Press on the "update" button on the screen, and then press "ok." You see a second identical image.

Step 3

Position your mouse on the top image and click on it. Make sure to press the mouse button down, and drag the top of the image off of the bottom image. The top image is brighter.

Step 4

Move the mouse to the top of the bottom image. Click on it and press the delete button on the keyboard. This action takes off the unwanted image.

Step 5

Proceed to save the design by clicking "file," and then click "save as." Make sure you save it under images.

Making Use of Sure Cuts a Lot

Step 1

Download "Provo Craft Design Studio Software," you can start off with the trial version, and it will update your computer's working system.

Step 2

Download the "Sure Cuts a Lot" software from the website. It costs about $60–$120 depending on the package you choose.

Step 3

Load and open the software on the computer.

Step 4

Put the foam, paper, or any other material you intend to cut on the Cricut mat and make sure it is well placed. Then, load the mat into the machine.

Step 5

Go to "file" and click on "import SVG." Locate the image and click on it. Click "open."

Step 6

To resize the image, click on one of the circles at the corner of the image and pull. You can also pull the image the other way if you intend to make it smaller.

Step 7

Locate the cut button above the image. On the tab, it is like a pair of scissors. Click it and the image cuts.

Chapter 6: Tools and Accessories You Need to Work with Cricut Maker Machine

It is very exciting when you consider the number of fun things you can do and all the supplies you'll have to get after purchasing a new Cricut machine. However, as much as it is exciting, it can also be overwhelming. From iron-on to cardstock, to vinyl, and foil, not to mention the mats, accessories, and tools. If care is not taken, you can spend as much on supplies as you did for the machine itself.

Before you proceed to buy these tools and accessories, you need to, first of all, ascertain their roles and importance. Below are lists of the tools and accessories you need to work with your Cricut Maker Machine:

Cutting Materials (Cardstock, Vinyl, Iron-On, Etc.)

i. Vinyl: If you intend to make stickers for cars, signs, tumblers, and coffee mugs, you'll need the following products:

- Printable Vinyl: Mainly used for making stickers

- Glitter Vinyl: Removable vinyl with sparkle

- Holographic Vinyl: It is the same with basic vinyl but comes in different colors depending on the angle that is being viewed

- Chalkboard Vinyl: Mainly used for making calendars and for labeling

- Removable Vinyl: Mostly used for temporary items that are not meant to last long, e.g., for rentals and others

- Permanent Vinyl: Used for projects that are intended to last long

- Dry Erase Vinyl: Used mainly for labeling

- Stencil Vinyl: Used for making screen-print shirts or hand-printed signs

- Patterned Vinyl: Used for fun design projects like Star Wars, Mickey Mouse, Minnie, watercolor, etc.

Some other items include:

Adhesive Foil: It is similar to vinyl. However, it is more complicated to use, thus, if you're new to working with vinyl, you should stick to basic vinyl for a start.

Transfer Tape: You need the tape to get your vinyl from the backing to your project.

ii. Iron-On: This is used to apply on hats, pillows, shirts, etc.

- Iron-On Designs: These are pre-made designs that can be used alone or customized with other types of iron-on

- Foil Iron-On: Used to add shine to your projects

- Glitter Iron-On: Used to add sparkle to projects; very easy to apply and weed

- Mesh Iron-On: Used to make jerseys

- SportFlex Iron-On: Stretchy iron-on used for athletic wears

- Holographic Iron-On: Used to add dimension to projects, either with holographic sparkle or opal holographic

- Everyday Iron-On: They can be used for most projects! They come in different bundles colors, and are highly versatile

- Patterned Iron-On: Used for creative designs like Star Wars, Mickey and Minnie, cute hippos, and watercolor. Basically, it is used to add fun designs to projects

iii. Felt: Used for making ornaments, finger puppets, headbands, and dress up masks.

iv. Cardstock: Used for scrapbooking, making gift boxes, gift bags, and cards.

v. Genuine Leather: Used for making home décor, accessories, and more.

vi. Fabric: Normally used for sewing projects.

vii. Faux Leather: Used for making baby moccasins, key chains, windows, and fringe.

viii. Infusible Ink: Used to create bold and permanent designs with pens and transfer sheets on the Cricut blanks including totes, shirts, coasters, and more.

ix. Window Cling: Used for short-term projects for fridges, windows, and other appliances.

Accessories (Pens, Tools, Mats, Etc.)

Mats: They come in two sizes; 12x24 and 12x12, and it is advisable to own at least one of each size. You will have to choose the type of mat to use, depending on the materials you will be cutting.

- Fabric Grip (Pink): used for fabric

- Light Grip (Blue): used for cardstock and paper projects

- Strong Grip (Purple): used for thick cardstock, poster board, and other thick materials

- Standard Grip (Green): used iron-on and vinyl

Pens: They are used for making gift tags and bags.

Tools: They are not mandatory, but they can make your work much easier if you have them:

- Scissors

- Scraper: Used to apply transfer tape on vinyl

- Spatula: Used to remove materials from the mat

- Weeder: Used to remove vinyl

- Bayer: this tool is used in ensuring that the fabric lays flat on the cutting mat

Precision Hand Tools: These are tools used during projects, especially after you've cut and weeded your projects.

- Acrylic Ruler: Used to cut straight lines and measure fabrics and other materials.

- Self-Healing Mat: This is a double-sided mat used for sewing, vinyl, iron-on or even paper project.

- TrueControl Knife: Used to easily cut thick, thin, delicate, and brittle materials. It is used to cut large sizes of fabric down to size mats.

- Cutting Ruler: This is a very large 18" ruler used for obtaining straight lines with cuts and placing designs on your blanks.

Specific Blades and Tools for Cricut Maker

Rotary Blade: It is included in the pack when you purchase the machine. The blade is used for cutting fabrics.

Knife Blade: It is used for cutting thick materials such as leather, basswood, balsa wood, chipboard, etc.

Scoring Wheel: It is used to make clean and crisp score lines.

Extras (EasyPress, Totes, BrightPad)

BrightPad: It is a tool used for weeding and a must-have for people that plan on using plenty of glitter or even those that work in low light areas.

EasyPress Mat: They are best used when applying iron-on. They trap the heat in materials so that iron-on can last long.

EasyPress & EasyPress 2: Are easy to use, portable heat presses. You need this item if you're going to be using a lot of iron-on. However, there's a slight difference between the EasyPress and the EasyPress 2.

Storage Totes: They are used for organizing, safeguarding the machine and other supplies. Below are three types of totes:

- Machine Tote: Used to hold cords and machines

- Rolling Storage Tote: Used to hold tools, EasyPress, laptop, Cuttlebug, cutting tools, and more

EasyPress Totes: Used to hold EasyPress machines, accessories, and other materials.

How to Clean a Cricut Maker

When the Cricut Maker was released by Cricut, it came with a new mat—the pink Fabric Grip mat. We all know that the Cricut Maker is a specialized machine for cutting fabric (among a host of other materials) and in order to ensure perfect fabric cuts, the mat has to be in top shape.

A lot of crafters find it difficult to keep their pink mats clean because it is different from the other mats used by the Explore Air series.

Do Not Use the Scraper

With the pink FabricGrip mat, there is no need to use the scraper because the adhesive on it is totally different from the others and can be scraped off the mat.

Keep Your Hands Off

Unlike other mats, the Cricut pink mat is made with delicate adhesive. Thus, if your hands are oily, they can easily break down the adhesive on the mat, resulting in the loss of its stickiness.

Be very careful with the mat and try as much as possible to avoid touching the adhesive. To adhere your fabric to the mat, use a Brayer and do not apply too much force, just enough to get you to stick to the mat. Another way of keeping your hands off the mat is by using tweezers to pick up pieces of materials from it. Desist from picking up a loose thread from the mat too—use tweezers, if you really must pick.

Threads Don't Matter

Talking about threads, whenever you cut the fabric, you'll realize that you end up with a lot of threads on the mat. Leave them. In our minds, we believe that our mats have to be super clean because any form of a bump when cutting vinyl or paper can be detrimental to our project. However, the rotary blade is super awesome; it can cut through loose threads, even if there is fabric over it—the cut won't be ruined at all.

Transfer Tape

If you are really worried about threads or maybe they are affecting your cuts, then you can opt to use transfer tape to take off the loose threads and other debris. Just place the sticky side down and peel it up. This option doesn't work all the time, so you're advised to use it with caution, and especially as a last resort.

Tips for the Felt

Cricut Maker cuts felt perfect. Thus, if you intend to embark on this operation, there are a couple of options available for you to avoid damaging your pink mat with fuzz. First of all, you can use the older green mats and take off your pink mat. However, the green mat should have some stick. It is better to gunk up the old mat than to gunk with the pink mat with sticky fiber. Save the pink mat for fabric.

You can opt to back your felt in transfer tape and stick that to the mat. You just have to peel it off after the cut. Depending on the material you're cutting, this option can be capital intensive because you'll be using transfer tape for every cut.

Pushing the Mat beyond Its Limits

As with every other thing, the Cricut mat has its limits. Thus, if you carry out a lot of intricate cutting with the rotary blade, you will realize that the mat begins to peel off. By default, the rotary blade wasn't designed to cut circles that are below ¾". Crafters that cut smaller circles than that even put further pressure on the blade and mat. Since the mat isn't designed to hand such pressure, it begins to peel off.

Do Not Re-Stick the Mat

On the internet, there are so many tutorials on how to re-stick the Cricut mat, and they involve the use of baby wipes, water, painter's tape, Goo Gone, spray adhesive, and many others. However, you have to understand that the pink mat's adhesive is completely different from the adhesive on other mats, and if you use any of those materials to re-stick it, you'll end up damaging your pink mat.

The pink mat's adhesive is designed to grip fabric but also release it easily. There is no viable method for re-sticking the pink mat. It is advisable to take proper care of your mat with the tips that have been given, as opposed to looking for means to restore a damaged mat.

Chapter 7: How to Use Design Space

How to Download Cricut Design Space

Visit design.cricut.com and click "download". When the download process is complete, you will have to open the file, depending on your computer or browser.

If you are using a Chrome browser, it will on your download bar, located at the bottom. Click to open and click run or next, as prompted.

Follow all the download prompts. You will have to accept the terms and conditions and click install. The procedure is straightforward and the prompts will walk you through everything. Finally, Design Space is downloaded, and it's time to explore.

You will be required to log in or create a username and password. Register your details on the website, and make sure you write down your login details, in case you log out in the future. Once you have taken care of that, click on a new project on the top right of the screen.

Before your machine can cut out projects, you will have to create your designs inside Design Space (also called Design Space canvas).

On the canvas, you will use the menu on the left side to kick off your designs.

- You will click upload to upload SVG files or images that you intend to cut. SVG is abbreviated for Scalable Vector Graphic and it is the most used file for cutting designs because it is explicit. SVG files can be found anywhere; you can find them on blogs, Etsy, and other places.

- The next menu on the left is Shapes. You can make use of stars, squares, circles, and other shapes to make your design. If you intend to scorecards or do other paper projects, you'll find score lines here.

- The third item on the left menu is Text. There are a number of things you can do with text, including: curving texts, making monograms, and using your personal fonts.

- The fourth item on the menu is Images. If you click the images' icon, you will be redirected to the designs you can use if you are subscribed to Cricut Access or the designs you can buy from Cricut if you have no subscription.

- Fifth on the left menu is Projects. If you click on projects, you will see a display of projects that are up for sale. However, there is another dropdown menu that you can use to select your projects. Your saved projects are also located in that area.

- Sixth on the left menu is Templates. Some crafters do not use this feature, but you can use them to ascertain the size of the design you intend to cut and how it is meant to look on a shirt or apron. Mind you, it is just a guide, thus, the actual template won't be cut out.

- Seventh on the left menu is the New+ button. If you want to start a new project, this is the menu to click. Always save your current project if you intend to keep it before starting a new one. The save button is located at the top right corner.

Cricut Design Space Top Menu

To understand Cricut Design Space, let's explore the top menu.

The top menu will only become available after you have texts typed out or a design uploaded. Thus, beginning from the left is the Undo button, used to rectify mistakes. The next button on the right is the Redo button, used to repeat and action.

The Deselect button is next, and it is used as the opposite of select. The Edit button is next and it has a dropdown menu that consists of copy or paste and flip. Next is the Size button; you can use it to change the actual size of your design or explore the bottom right of the design to use the two-way directional arrow.

Right at the bottom left of the canvas is the unlock button. This feature consists of a four-way directional arrow used to widen designs without making them taller or making them taller without making them wider.

Next on the menu is the rotation tool, used to rotate designs to every degree possible. The last feature on the top menu is the x and y coordinates, used to position designs on the canvas.

How to Weld

It can be a little bit daunting for a Cricut Space beginner to use the weld tool, however, when you become proficient, it'll open the doors to many more projects because it is a tool that will be used often.

The weld tool is located at the bottom right corner of Design Space, under the layers panel. Other tools close to it are: flatten, contour, and slice tools.

In Cricut Design Space, the weld tool does the following:

- Connects cursive text and scrip in order for it to cut as a single word instead of individual letters

- Merge multiple layers and shapes into a single layered image

- Take off cut lines from different shapes and cut them as one big image

i. For you to use weld, the text or shapes you intend to weld together must be touching or overlapping each other.

ii. To select the layers you intend to weld together, select a layer, hold down 'Ctrl' and select the other layer. After selecting both layers, click 'weld.' If you intend to weld the whole layers on your canvas, click 'select all' to select all the layers and click 'weld.'

iii. If you weld different layers together, it becomes a single image and will cut out in one color and on one mat.

Without selecting multiple layers, the weld option will not be available for use.

In order to weld texts, you have to make sure that the letters are all touching each other. Thus, you have to reduce the spacing of the letters until they begin to touch each other. Once you do this, you can select everything and click weld.

How to Slice

The slice tool is a feature in Cricut Design Space that cuts one design element out of another. You can use it to cut text from a shape, cut one shape from another shape, or cut overlapping shapes from each other. Below is an example, and we will cut text out from a heart shape:

i. Choose a font

Use any font you prefer, but decrease your letter spacing to 0.9 so that your letters link together.

ii. Weld the text

When you're done with the spacing, you have to transform your letters into a single image by using the weld tool. When you weld your letters, it permanently connects all the design elements into one image.

iii. Choose an SVG

You can find a heart SVG from lovesvg.com. You just need to ungroup everything and simply delete the unwanted elements.

iv. Set the size of your design

You need to resize the image. Depending on the size you want, simply type the intended size on the width box. For this example, we'll stick to 5.5 inches.

v. Arrange the design

You need to arrange the text and heart by clicking 'arrange.'

vi. Use the slice tool

When you have arranged your design perfectly, select your text, and hold down the 'Ctrl' key, select the heart and click 'slice.' Now, you can remove the text from the heart and delete.

vii. Once your design is done, it is time to cut vinyl

How to Flatten

The flatten tool is a feature used to turn multi-layered images into a single-layered image.

What Does Flatten Do in Cricut Design Space?

Flatten is a tool that turns multi-layered images into a single-layered image. The tool is used in the making of decals, labels, stickers, and much more. You can flatten multiple layers of SVG cut files into single-layered images, before printing and cutting.

With the flatten tool, you can achieve the following:

- Remove cut lines from an image

- Transform multi-layered images into a single-layered image

- Used to transfer regular images into printable images for print-and-cut

- Used to maintain distinct colors of multi-layered images

Using the flatten tool:

- To select the layers you intend to flatten together, click 'select all' or hold down 'Ctrl' and select the layers

- After selecting, click flatten at the bottom right corner

- When you do that, the image is now flattened

How to Attach

Basically, there are two distinct reasons for using the attach tool:

- To keep scoring/writing lines in the right place

- To keep shapes in the correct place on the mat as on the canvas

Using the Attach Tool to Maintain the Same Arrangement

If you want all the pieces of your project to remain in the exact location during cutting, as it is on your CDS canvas, you have to:

- Select all the items of each color

- Click 'attach' at the lower right corner

- Repeat the process for each color layer until they are all nested under a label that says "attach"

With the attach tool, you will be able to cut out your projects exactly the way you arranged them on your Cricut canvas.

How to Group/Ungroup

Group on Cricut Design Space means to group two or more layers into one layer. On the other hand, ungroup means breaking up a layer group into separate layers. There are different types of group layers, and if a layer is grouped multiple times, you will have to ungroup them multiple times in order to completely separate them.

Group: To group, you have to select the layers you intend to group together by clicking your mouse and dragging on the design or select multiple layers in your layer panel by using a keyboard shortcut. To select multiple layers, you have to press 'Ctrl' and select your layers on your computer. After selection, you have to click right on your mouse and click the Group button. If you wish, there is also the option of creating multiple groups within groups, it makes it easier to deal with complex designs.

In Design Space, groups work better with layers, especially when you're trying to manipulate some parts of a design. With Group, you can easily resize or stretch the selection.

Ungroup: It is very easy to ungroup designs that are grouped together. To ungroup, you need to select the layer you intend to ungroup, click right on your mouse, and click on the "Ungroup" button or select "Ungroup." There are layers that might have been grouped multiple times, thus, if you intend to completely Ungroup, you have to continuously select again and again, and keep clicking Ungroup, until it's completely done.

The primary reason for using the ungroup feature is to change or manipulate some part of a design. The change could be physical, or it could be manipulating some parts of a design by welding, attaching, or using some other methods, without touching on the rest of the design.

How to Duplicate/Delete

If you intend to duplicate a layer or set of layers, you have to select the part of the design or the layers you intend to duplicate, click right on your mouse, and click the Duplicate button.

On the other hand, if you intend to delete a single layer or a set of layers, you have to select the part of the design or the layers you intend to delete, click right on your mouse, and select the Delete button.

If you have two designs and you intend to retain only one, select the design you intend to delete, click right on your mouse, and click the Delete option.

How to Color Sync

As you finish making up a project in Cricut Design Space, it is possible that by the time you go over to cut it, you are faced with four different mats with different shades of black. The reason for such result lies with the fact that you may have used several images from the images tab, all being with slightly different shades of similar colors. In order to overcome this, go up into the top right-hand corner under the green button marked 'Make It.' You will find the option 'Color Sync.' By clicking on it, you will allow the function to pull up every single item on your project to be sorted out by similar color groups.

Here is an example whereby six different shades of green emerge. Consequently, Color Sync will identify six different shades of green, making six different green cutting mats as you make your project. If the final result of your project is to have multiple shades, then there is no need to modify anything. However, if you wish to streamline in order to obtain one green cutting mat, all you have to do is to select items and drag them into different colors. By doing this, you avoid going into each individual layer through a manual change of color. On the other hand, if the purpose is to modify the color in order to obtain one shade, like for instance, if you want to put together similar colors to one mat, then select the color shade bar situated on the left-hand side and pull that into the color you want to switch into. This option allows us to streamline different colors of cutting mats to only a few. The choice is yours.

Using Text in Cricut Design Space

Once you sign into Cricut Design Space, select one of the three places marked with arrows to start a new project. Then click the three-line icon on the top left to proceed for a 'New Project.' As you start a new project, you will be directed to a gridded design space called a Canvas. Select the left sidebar that contains the text icon. A small box will emerge, shown by a second arrow, in which you can enter your text. Once the text is entered, choose a font that can be found on the far left arrow. You will quickly notice how the cursive font has large spaces between the letters.

To remedy this and bring the letters closer together, modify the letter space to a smaller one (negative numbers can also be used to reach the effect needed).

Getting Started with Text

Start typing your text by simply clicking the text icon located on the left toolbar. A text box will appear in which you can start inserting your text. Font, style, and size, as well as line spacing and letter spacing, can be selected by going on the top toolbar. It is advisable to type your text first and then make the changes you want afterward.

Fonts

The function 'Font' will display a diversity of fonts to choose from. You have the option to see only your fonts by clicking on the system or by clicking on Cricut. If you have a preferred font in mind, then use the search option. Finally, you have the option to filter the fonts if you look for a writing or multilayer font.

How to Add Your Own Fonts

If you rather prefer to add your own fonts, then sites are available, such as creativemarket.com, thehungryjpeg.com, or dafont.com, which will offer a large selection to choose from.

Creating your own items to be sold requires that the font comes with a commercial license. After having selected the font, you want to work with, find the file on your computer, and open it. As fonts come in a zip file, it is required to open the extract files which has been opened very likely automatically. Once the files are extracted, variations of the font will be displayed as 'Original,' 'Italics,' and 'Bold.' It is not necessary to install all the variations as often the 'Original' can easily be modified in your design software. In addition, two versions called 'Open Type Font' and 'TrueType Font' are offered. Their installation depends very much on the system you use. So, try both. Once the file you want is selected, click right on it and install it. The new font chosen will appear under 'System Fonts' in the Design Space. While in the process of installing a new font, it is advisable to close Design Space and re-open it to see your new font.

How to Access Special Characters

You can access special characters by using Humble Script, which provides many options. You can access it by typing 'character map' in your system search box. The app will appear. A drop-down menu indicates which font you are working with. Secure the option 'Advanced View' is properly checked. Then modify the character set to Unicode and finally group by Unicode subrange. At this stage, a new box will appear for the Unicode subrange. Scroll it all the way to the bottom and select 'Private Use Characters.'

In regards to your design place, if you wish to delete a letter from your text box and have it replaced, then hit 'Ctrl' plus the 'V' key at the same time to paste your new special character. The configuration will look like a square, but the text will change. If you wish to change the size, just use the font size on the top toolbar. Once you are satisfied with the final result in terms of the sizing and spacing of your text, just highlight and select. Then click the align button on the top toolbar. If you wish, you can choose to align your text either to the left or center it or align it to the right.

How to Curve Text

Curving text is rather simple to achieve in Design Space as it consists mainly to slide the text to the left. By doing so, your text will curve up. Once this is done, you can use the letter-spacing option if you need to make adjustments. Finally, you can select everything and center your lines.

How to Make a Stencil

Great for hand-painted signs, stencils in Design Space can be created with the shapes tool on the left toolbar. By clicking on the unlock button situated on the bottom left, you can stretch your shape into a rectangle. Insert the text you want on your stencil, with or without the tips referred earlier in regards to centering, spacing, sizing, curving, or fonts. Once you are satisfied with the final result, highlight, select all the text, and click the attach button on the bottom right toolbar. Select both the text and the box, followed by selecting the align tool on the top toolbar. You can select align horizontally and then select align vertically. This will center your text within the box. While both your text and box are still selected, click the attach button on the bottom right toolbar. At this stage, your wording will change to the same color as your box, with the cut line still visible. As everything is combined together, you can be ready to proceed to make a stencil.

How to Use Contour with Text

Contour is used to delete or hide unwanted pieces of a design or image. To use the contour tool, you have to select the image or layer (one at a time) you intend to edit and click on the contour tool located at the end of the layers panel.

By default, it is impossible to use the contour tool on text, and one of the reasons is that text is dependent on the font itself. Thus, the program will reject any excessive modification involved with the contour.

You have to weld your text before you can use the contour feature, and to do this, select the text or word you intend to use and click the weld button at the bottom of the Layers panel.

After welding, you'll be able to contour your texts or words and do away with the letters or blank spaces that you intend to discard.

Remember to save a copy of your text if you intend to use it in the future, because after you weld it, you won't be able to edit it afterward.

How to Edit Images in Cricut Design Space Using the Slice Tool

You can use the slice tool to edit images in Cricut Design Space. To do so, these are the following steps:

- Add your uploaded image to your canvas in Cricut Design Space. To do this, click on the image and click on insert images. The program allows users to upload more than one image at a time to the canvas.

- To work on your project, you have to expand the size of the image by clicking the right bottom corner and dragging it down a little. Do it until you can clearly see all the elements of the image.

- If there is any part of the image you intend to get rid of, you can use the slice tool to cut it off. On the left side toolbox, click on Shapes, then click on the square.

- Click on the left bottom circle under the square to unlock it. If you see a lock icon, click on it. When you do this, you've successfully unlocked the square, thus, you can move it in any shape you want by using the right bottom circle. You can use the square to replace the deleted part of the image.

- With the square highlighted, press and hold the shift button. Click the bubble image with your mouse. This action highlights both of them.

- With both the image and square highlighted, use your mouse to click the slice tool at the bottom right corner.

- Pull away the pieces of your slice and delete if you want.

- Go on with the process until you successfully edit the image.

Chapter 8: Design Space Software Secrets and the Design Space App

(The Basics of the Cricut Software)

I guess you just bought a new Cricut machine, and you are wondering how you are going to start in Design Space. This is a common feeling among newcomers and it can be overwhelming, to say the least. However, once you learn the basics, you'll realize that CDS is not so hard to use because it is user-friendly. Below are some Design Space software secrets:

1. **Cricut Access** – Newcomers using Cricut for the first time get a free trial of Cricut Access. When you start your trial, you should put in enough effort to explore every aspect, so that you can make up your mind on whether to continue or not. Cricut Access plans start from $7.99/month, and it contains a vast library of images, projects, and fonts. If you are serious about your designing in Cricut Design Space, then this is the easiest way for you to get started.

2. **Ready to Make Projects** – When you make 'ready to make projects,' all you are doing is throwing guesswork out of the window. Cricut machines always come with a number of projects that show you exactly how to make them. In some instances, you can even edit the design by adding personalization or changing the size.

3. **Cricut Community Projects** – They are finished projects that can be used by anyone on the platform. There are different ways to access community projects; you can buy some while some others are included in the Cricut Access subscription. Furthermore, you're advised to share your awesome works with other community crafters, especially if your project was designed using Cricut Access.

4. **Cricut Design Space App** – There is a Cricut app that can be downloaded on mobile devices (Android and Apple). With this app, you can work with Cricut Design Space on your

mobile devices like iPad and tablets, to design and then connect to a Cricut cutting machine.

5. **Canvas** – This is the screen that is used for designing. If you intend to start a new project on the Design Space landing page, just click the "new project" button and the canvas will open up.

On the bottom left corner, there is a zoom in and out button you can use to inspect the big picture or tiny details of your design. Whereas, on the left-hand side you'll find the following buttons:

a) New: Used to start new projects

b) Projects: Used to open all projects in Cricut Design Space

c) Templates: Used to check how a particular project will work on different items. There is the possibility of changing the size and colors of any chosen template.

d) Images: This is where you'll find all the images you have uploaded and the ones you can buy from Cricut Access.

e) Upload: Used to upload JPEG, SVG, or PNG saved in your computer or mobile device.

f) Text: Used to select fonts for design projects.

g) Shapes: Involves basic score lines and shapes. Crafters use a combination of shapes to make different designs.

Purchase Materials One at a Time: If you already have a number of linked cartridges, or you are not ready to subscribe with Cricut Access, you can simply buy files from time to time. Remember, any file you purchase becomes yours for life, thus, you can use it on any project of your choice.

- Make sure you set up your payment method under the 'account settings' on the left-hand side because Cricut Design Space will prompt you for payment before you're allowed to cut your file.

6. **Filters**: You will save yourself a lot of time and stress on Design Space if you know exactly what you're looking for. If you are in search of any image or text in particular, you should use the filters to narrow things down to items available on Cricut Access or to the ones you have uploaded.

7. **Upload Your Own Image**: If you intend to make personalized gifts and items, you should endeavor to upload your own images. With Cricut Design Space, it is extremely easy to upload saved images on the computer and use print-and-cut or cut them out. If you're a crafter that sells items, make it a priority to check for images that are copyrighted and never use them. Google is your best friend, thus, you can always research on laws surrounding copyright infringement. There are a number of companies that actively prosecute defaulters and Disney is one of them. Be extremely careful.

8. **Preview Screen**: The recent update carried out by Cricut Design Space has made it possible to move things around with the preview screen before cutting. The Cricut software tries to save as much material as possible, but sometimes the cuts come out with huge blank gaps in between. However, you have the option of manually cutting those blank spaces.

9. **General Editing Tools**: Cricut Design Space editing tools are quite straightforward. They make it very easy for crafters to easily make their designs, and these tools are found on the lower right corner of the CDS:

    o **Attach** – Used to attach messages or texts to make sure they cut out the same way they look on the canvas.

    o **Slice** – Used to slice objects, to make split letter monograms, and to cut images out of others.

    o **Contour** – Delete outside or inside of unwanted lines or images

    o **Weld** – Used to join objects into one object and weld cursive texts into one continuous line.

    o **Flatten** – Used to flatten images together before printing

On the upper right corner of Cricut Design Space, you'll find the following:

- **Color Sync** – Used to ascertain the number of colors you have on your canvas. By dragging and dropping items in this panel, you can change items to the same color.

- **Layers Panel** – Used to check the different layers of your images. If you click the eye, you will hide certain layers, and if you click again, you'll unhide them.

It may seem daunting at first, but the more you explore the software, the more you will get grounded with it.

Chapter 9: Best Projects You Can Do with Cricut Maker

1. Vinyl Decals and Stickers

One of the projects you can carry out with the Cricut Maker is cutting vinyl and stickers.

You just have to create your design in Cricut Design Space, instruct the Maker to cut, then weed, and transfer the design to whatever surface you choose.

2. Fabric Cuts

The presence of the Rotary Blade in the Cricut Maker makes it a well-respected machine. The Maker can cut any type of fabric, including: chiffon, denim, silk, and even heavy canvas. With this machine, you can definitely cut huge amounts of fabrics without using any backup, and this is because it comes equipped with a fabric cutting mat. Awesome machine!

3. Sewing Patterns

One major benefit of owning the Cricut Maker machine is the extensive library of sewing patterns that you'll have access to.

The library has hundreds of patterns, including some from Riley Blake Designs and Simplicity; all you need to do is select the pattern you want and the machine will do the cutting.

4. Balsa Wood Cuts

The knife blade, coupled with the 4 kg force of the machine, means that the Cricut Maker can easily cut through thick materials (up to 2.4 mm thick). With these features, thick materials that were off-limits for earlier Cricut machines are now being done.

5. Thick Leather Cuts

Just like balsa wood, the Cricut Maker is also used for thick leather cuts.

6. Homemade Cards

Paper crafters use the Cricut Maker because the power and precision of the machine make the cutting of cards and paper far quicker and easier. With the machine, homemade cards just got better.

7. Jigsaw Puzzles

With the Cricut Maker, crafters can make jigsaw puzzles because the knife blade cuts through much thicker materials than ever before.

8. Christmas Tree Ornaments

Cricut machine owners can easily make Christmas tree ornaments. All you have to do is go through the sewing library for Christmas patterns, use any fabric of your choice to cut out the pattern, and sew them together. Remember, the rotary blade cuts through all sorts of fabric.

9. Quilts

Thanks to the partnership between Cricut and Riley Blake Designs, Cricut Design Space now has a number of quilting patterns in the sewing pattern gallery.

The Cricut Maker is now used to cut quilting pieces with high precision before they are sewn together.

10. Felt Dolls and Soft Toys

The "felt dolls and clothes" pattern is one of the simplest designs in the sewing pattern library. Thus, it is used for homemade dolls and toys.

The process is easy; just select the pattern you want, cut, and then sew.

11. T-shirt Transfers

The Cricut Maker is used for cutting out heat transfer vinyl for crafters to transfer their designs to fabric. To achieve this, you have to make your design in Design Space, load the machine with your heat transfer vinyl, cut the material, and then iron the transfer onto the T-shirt. Alternatively, you can use the Cricut EasyPress to transfer the vinyl.

12. Baby Clothes

The Cricut Maker cannot cut adult clothing patterns because the mat size is only 12" x 24". However, you can easily make baby clothing patterns with the machine.

13. Doll Clothes

Just like baby clothes, the Cricut Maker can easily make doll clothing patterns because the mat size is big enough.

14. Fabric Appliqués

The bonded fabric blade doesn't come with the Cricut Maker, but if you buy it, you will be able to use your machine to cut complex fabric designs like appliqué. For the bonded fabric blade to cut effectively, there has to be bonded backing on the material.

15. Calligraphy Signs

The stand out feature of the Cricut Maker is the Adaptive Tool System. With this feature, the machine will remain relevant in the foreseeable future because it fits with all the blades and tools of the explore series, as well as all future blades and tools made by Cricut.

The calligraphy pen is one of such tools, and it is ideal for sign and card making.

16. Jewelry Making

For crafters that like to explore jewelry making, the power of the Cricut Maker means that you can cut thicker materials, and while you can't cut things like diamonds, silver, or gold, you can definitely try to make a beautiful pair of leather earrings.

17. Wedding Invitations and Save the Dates

Weddings are capital intensive and we all know how the so-called 'little' expenses like save the dates and invitations can add up to the huge cost. However, if you have the Cricut Maker machine, then you can make your invitations and save the dates yourself.

The Maker is capable of making invitations of the highest quality. It cuts out intricate paper designs and the calligraphy pen is very useful too.

18. Wedding Menus, Place Cards, and Favor Tags

The Cricut Maker is not restricted to the production of pre-wedding invitations and save the dates. With the machine, you can also produce other items such as place cards, wedding menus, favor tags, etc.

In order to keep the theme front and center, the crafter is advised to use a similar design for all their stationery.

19. Coloring Book

With the Cricut Maker, you can make 'mindful coloring' books from scratch. To achieve this goal, you need a beautiful design, a card, and paper. Then you command the Cricut Maker to create your personal and completely unique coloring book with the aid of the fine-point pen tool.

20. Coasters

In the sewing library, there are a number of beautiful coaster patterns and as such, the Maker is used to coasters.

With the Cricut Machine, you can work with materials such as metallic sheets, quilt, leather, and everything in between.

21. Fabric Keyrings

The Cricut Maker makes fabric keyrings and the process is simple—it cuts out the pattern and then you sew it together. Besides, there are a number of designs for fabric keyrings in the sewing pattern library.

22. Headbands and Hair Decorations

The Cricut Maker is known to cut through materials like thick leather and this has gone on to inspire the production of intricate headbands and hair decorations. The machine is so inspiring; crafters in the fashion world use it for creative designs and projects.

23. Cut-Out Christmas Tree

It is a normal tradition for people to buy Christmas trees during the holiday season. However, if you don't have enough space for a big tree in your living room, or maybe you're allergic to pine, then you can definitely create your own Christmas tree.

The production of an interlocking wooden tree is something the Cricut Maker does easily because the blade is capable of cutting through thick materials like wood. With the Cricut Maker, you don't use a laser.

24. Cake Toppers

When Cricut bought over the cake cutter machine, the idea was to create shapes made of gum paste, fondant, and others.

It is obvious that the Cricut Maker can't cut as good as the cake machine; however, it can be used to produce tiny and intricate paper designs that can be used to decorate cakes.

25. Fridge Magnets

Cricut machines like the Maker and Explore Air are capable of cutting out magnetic materials. Thus, crafters can use the Maker to make those fancy magnetic designs placed on refrigerators.

26. Window Decals

If you're one of those who love to display inspiring quotes on your windows or even fancy little patterns on your car, then the Maker got you covered.

You just have to load the Maker with window cling and get your design created.

27. Scrapbooking Embellishments

The Cricut Maker is used for embellishments when scrapbooking. It is public knowledge that Cricut machines are super when it comes to cutting intricate designs. However, the Cricut Maker takes it to a whole new level, and the responsive new blades take away all forms of complexity.

28. Craft Foam Cuts

In the past, Cricut machines found it difficult to cut craft foam (especially the Explore Machines); however, the Cricut Maker, with the 4 kg of force, cuts through craft foam very easy.

29. Boxes and 3D Shapes

The Cricut machines come with a scoring stylus and this tool can create items with the sharpest edges imaginable.

We all know that the Cricut Maker can execute all kinds of sewing patterns thrown at it. It can also cut paper crafts, including 3D shapes and boxes.

30. Stencils

The Maker comes in handy for people that create things that are used to create other items. The machine is incredible for making stencils, bearing in mind that you can utilize thicker materials to create the stencils.

31. Temporary Tattoos

If you're one of those people that want to have tattoos, but don't want them permanent for life, then the Cricut Maker is your go-to machine.

With the Cricut Maker, you can etch your design on a tattoo paper (mostly coated with transfer film) and use it on your skin.

32. Washi Tape

Crafters that use Washi tape for scrapbooking can testify to how expensive it can be, especially when buying bulk from craft stores. However, those who own the Cricut machine can use it to cut out Washi sheets—they can print-and-cut their personal designs on it.

33. Addressed Envelopes

The Cricut Maker is an astounding machine that can save you from spending on certain items. Remember, we talked about making handmade wedding invitations; with the Cricut

Machine, you can also make envelopes to go with the cards. Another good feature about the machine is that it is equipped with a calligraphy pen and a fine-point pen, meaning that it is capable of addressing your envelopes automatically. All you need to do is make sure that the words are clear enough for the postman to read.

34. Glassware Decals

With a Cricut Maker, you can cut vinyl to make glassware designs. People who host themed parties will love this one, e.g., if you're hosting a summer house party and you're serving mojitos, you can decorate your drinking glasses with coconuts and palm tree decals. Also, people holding Xmas parties can design and cut themed stickers to use on their cups.

35. Decorations

There are a couple of other desktop craft machines that are used to create general household decorations, but the Cricut Maker is one of the best—if not the very best.

With the Cricut Maker, you'll be empowered to create 3D wall hangings, beautiful cut-outs in the living room, and even things like signage in your closets, etc.

36. Cushion Transfers

With your Cricut Maker, you can brighten up your cushion and pillows by adding your homemade designs. With the flocked iron-on vinyl, you can create a lovely textured cushion using heat transfer vinyl on the Cricut machine.

37. 3D Bouquet

The machine takes us back to the wedding theme once more.

Remember, with intuitive tools like the scoring stylus and the fine-point; the Cricut Maker is superbly equipped to carry out intricate paper crafts. Thus, you can introduce a touch of homemade crafts to your wedding, or even create flowers to design your home, knowing that you don't have to water them.

With the Cricut Maker, you can have yourself a lovely, beautiful, and immortal bouquet.

38. Gift Tags

We all know that gift tags consume some of our money during the holiday season. However, with your Cricut Maker, you don't have to buy them anymore; you can just make your own.

39. Clutch Bags and Purses

The sewing pattern library is awesome; thus you can make different types of full-size purses, coin purse, and even clutch bags.

Chapter 10: Best Projects You Can Do with Explore Air 2

1. Cricut Patterned Vinyl T-shirt

The patterned Cricut iron-on pack allows you to create three different patterned iron-on sheets on a T-shirt design. The following tips will help you create this T-shirt: you will need to use the free dress SVG linked above, use glitter and patterned HTV without making them touch, and finally, use heat resistant tape to keep vinyl in place.

2. Reverse Canvas Cricut Explore Project

This technique is another Cricut project with free SVG. To realize the project is advisable to take your time as it may take 48 hours or more to realize. You can contrast bold colors and you will have to ensure that the paint is dry before heat pressing (or use adhesive vinyl instead).

3. A Baby Bodysuit Cricut Project

You can make baby bodysuits with glitter heat transfer vinyl. To realize a perfect baby bodysuit, use the heat press pillow for best results, use Siser glitter HTV, and use weeding boxes to make weeding glitter easier.

4. Stainless Steel Water Bottles

With this new and standing Cricut machine project, you can realize an impressive custom stainless steel water bottles. The adhesive vinyl makes the stainless steel look really stunning.

To realize Cricut Explore Air projects satisfactorily, you will need to get yourself familiar with how to apply the vinyl to curved surfaces, choose a stylish font to match the surface and to use duplicate corner squares to align the design with multiple colors.

5. Cricut Slice Tool Project

Realize a baby onesie using a Cricut slice tool project idea; you will utilize the slice tool that will cut text or other design elements out of larger designs. This is a great idea if you have really pretty vinyl and you want to expand your skill. To accomplish this project, you will have to think about using Siser foil HTV or use another quality heat transfer vinyl that does not peel. Do not forget that you will be weeding out what you would usually be keeping!

6. Save the Date Card Project

To realize this project successfully, you will have to use Cricut pens and Cricut light grip mats. The mat will enable you to avoid damaging light products such as paper envelopes. The Design Space app will provide you with plenty of prompts. When removing cardstock from the mat, you will have to bend the mat away rather than the card. Use the same font used on the card to write the address on the envelope. With a ruler on the side of the mat, you can determine how large your fonts need to be. You can address more than one envelope at a time since you can fit as many as you can on the mat. Finally, use your Cricut to cut photo borders into different shapes.

7. Cricut Reverse Canvas Project

For this project, you will have to get yourself a canvas that can easily be available on Amazon. With a craft knife, cut away the canvas from the frame or use a staple remover to pull the staples out. If you wish, you can color or paint the frame once the canvas has been removed. This is optional; however, it is advisable to use adhesive vinyl rather than iron-on if you want to paint your canvas first. This project uses Cricut foil iron-on. A selection of fonts is available as shown in the video, such as 'hello there,' which is under the font called 'Bickley Script,' or 'handsome,' which is under the font called 'Classic Roman Std Reg.' Those are the Cricut fonts available in Design Space. To reapply the canvas to the frame, use a hot glue gun (as shown in the video) or a staple gun. Finally, apply Command Velcro strips to hang your canvas.

8. Custom Pillow Cases with Cricut HTV

To accomplish a custom pillowcase, you will need a weeding tool to make it quick and easy. An ironing mat is strongly suggested as a good surface to press your iron-on vinyl. Whereas Cricut iron-on is applied with heat and is used primarily for clothing and other fabrics, Cricut vinyl works like a sticker that can be applied on pretty much any surface without being pressed on with heat. The blue light grip or green standard grip mat will allow you to cut Cricut iron-on vinyl. Then, just need to set the temperature on your iron to the appropriate setting for the fabric you are pressing onto. It is possible that over time, the vinyl may start to lift. Just simply apply your iron to press it back into position.

9. Custom Tote Bag

By following Carly Hall's tutoring session, you will learn how to make a tote bag with the Cricut Explore Air 2. This project is to realize a Halloween tote bag. The step-by-step of this project is applicable to any other design. To successfully accomplish a custom tote bag is suggested that you use the Cricut Explore Air 2 (color mint). Use the Design Space app for iPhone. Equally, you can use a beta app for Android, which can be downloaded from the Play Store or use the computer software. Vinyl designs are available on Amazon for blank tote bags.

10. Working with Patterns in Design Space – Making a Star Ornament

Like the Halloween tote described above, the process remains identical and can be used to make ornaments for any occasion. You will need wool felt as it is the best material to utilize to make the ornament casing. Cut it with the rotary blade made only for the Cricut Maker. Alternatively, you can use stiffer felt, which will be cut by the deep cut blade of other machines such as the Explore Air 2. It is advisable to use the pink mat as it is a fabric grip mat. You will then use the EasyPress. Finally, use a hot glue gun to stick the two sides of felt together. Your project is now completed.

Chapter 11: Tips and Tricks to Make Cricut Machines Easier and Efficient

The Cricut Maker and Explore Air 2 are great machines that can be used to do a lot of things. However, new and first-time owners find it a little challenging to get their heads over the machines, making it difficult for them to utilize the machines to their full potentials.

For crafters that get little or no support from experienced users, it takes quite some time for them to really get a hold of the machines and finally maximize their output.

If you've purchased or intend to purchase a Cricut machine, then you must know that there are tips and tricks you can apply to boost the machine's output and ensure optimum functionality.

Most of the tips are geared towards helping beginners understand their Cricut machines; however, there are also other advanced tips for veterans. Below are some of the tips and tricks:

- **Make Sure You Subscribe to Cricut Access**

If you own a Cricut Explore Air 2, you have to subscribe to Cricut Access in order to get the best out of it. There are two subscription plans—the yearly plan and the monthly plan.

Having an active subscription plan with Cricut Access will save you a lot of money because you won't have to buy individual projects and images. With Cricut Access, you'll have access to thousands of projects and over 375 fonts. Plus, it's less stressful to pay a flat than to always worry about the amount of money you'll be spending on projects.

- **Always De-tack Your Cutting Mat**

The Cricut Maker comes with the blue light grip mat, while the Explore Air 2 normally comes with the green standard cutting mat. Before putting on the machine, make sure you always place your materials onto the mat first.

When you buy the Explore Air 2, the green mat that comes with it is very sticky. Thus, as a reward for your first project, peel off the plastic cover and place a clean, dry T-shirt over the mat.

Even with the right tools, it can be very difficult to get off the cardstock when it's new, and this results in damaged projects sometimes. The blue light grip mat doesn't have such problems; thus, instead of de-tacking the green mat, you can purchase it for your card and paper projects.

- **Make Sure You Keep Your Cutting Mat Covers**

New cutting mats always come with a plastic shield that covers them, and they are easily pulled off and on. Whatever you do, make sure you don't misplace the cover, and always put it back on the mat whenever you're done using it—this practice helps to keep the mat sticky and clean for over longer periods.

- **Make Sure You Clean the Cutting Mat**

Whenever you use your cutting mat, make sure you clean it afterward, and it is recommended that you use nonalcoholic baby wipes. If you do this consistently, it'll reduce the buildup of vinyl and cardstock residue, as well as dust stains and other regular lint that float about.

- **Make Sure You Acquire the Right Tools**

To fully maximize the Cricut machine experience, you have acquired the Cricut toolset. The set contains a scraper, a weeding tool, a spatula, and scissors. If your craft involves cutting either heat transfer vinyl or adhesive vinyl, then the weeding tool is a must. The other tools come in handy for different activities and projects.

- **Purchase the Scoring Stylus**

The scoring stylus is mandatory for a whole lot of card projects. Thus, without it, your options will be limited, and it doesn't come with the machine at purchase. However, if you buy your machine as part of a bundle, there's a high probability that it'll be included, so you need to check.

- **Your First Project Should Be Your Sample Project**

As a beginner, who just bought the Cricut machine, your first project should be the sample project. When you purchase the Explore Air 2, you'll realize that the machine is loaded with sample cardstock for users to make their first cards. The supporting materials are minimal and it is just one card. Thus, instead of embarking on a huge and fancy project, you can embark on a simple project so that you can get a feel of how things work—hardware and software-wise.

- **Test Cuts**

Before you carry out any serious project, make sure to do a test cut first, because there are a number of things that can possibly go wrong. For example, if you set the blade too high, it might not cut the cardstock or vinyl properly. Also, if you set the blade too low, it could possibly ruin the cutting mat. Executing a test cut involves checking the settings of the machine and asking the machine to cut a small circle, maybe.

- **Make Sure You Always Replace Pen Lids after Use**

A lot of crafters have the habit of forgetting their pen inside the machine when they're done with their projects. It can happen to anyone but make sure the pen ink doesn't dry out; it is important to get the lid on it as soon as you're done with your project. The Cricut pen is very expensive, and maybe that's the reason why Design Space always prompts users to get their lids back on.

- **You Should Link Your Old Cartridges to Your Design Space Account**

If you have any Cricut cartridges from a previous Cricut machine; you can link them up to your new account. The procedure is fast and simple; however, you have to understand that each cartridge can only be linked once. Thus, if you intend to buy a used cartridge, you have to confirm that it hasn't been linked to another account already.

- **Getting Materials off the Cutting Mat**

Rather than using conventional tools for removing vinyl or cardstock from the cutting mat, you can consider another method. When people peel their projects from the mat, it can possibly result in curling; thus, you should peel the mat away from the project instead. In addition, you should also do the unconventional method of bending the mat away from the card.

When you do this, the mat might turn upside down and bend one corner to leave the cardstock. At this stage, you can just place the spatula under to take off your project. Some people use their credit cards to take off the mat, and as much as this might work, it can also damage the adhesive on the mat.

- **Purchase the Deep Cut Blade**

One of the most painful things in the world of crafting is embarking on a project without the right tools. Unlike the Maker, you need to have the deep cut blade for the Explore Air 2 to be able to cut through thicker leather, card, chipboard, and others. When you order the blade, you should also order the blade housing too. Furthermore, you don't have to wait till you need it urgently before you order for it. Buy it today.

• Use Free SVG Files in Order to Cut the Cost

In terms of designing projects, you don't have to be fully dependent on the Design Space store. You have other options; there's the option of creating your personal SVG files or using some other free SVG files on the internet. There are a number of websites on the internet that have so many free SVG files. All you have to do in order to locate them is to carry out minimal research on the internet.

• Make Sure You Load the Mat Properly

Before you start cutting, you must be sure that your mat is loaded properly. It must be placed under the rollers. If the mat is not loaded properly, the machine may not cut at all, or in other cases, it might start cutting before the top of the grip on the mat.

• Different Pens Work in the Explore Air 2

The Cricut pens are not the only ones that work in the Explore Air 2 machine. Examples of other pens that can work with the machine include, but not limited to, American Craft Pens and Sharpie Pens. With that said, you should have it at the back of your mind that Cricut pens are of the highest quality and are known to last longer than others.

- **Make Use of Free Front for Some of Your Projects**

On the internet, there are a number of websites where you can get free fonts to use for your designs. To do this, you need to visit the sites and download the fonts, install them to your system and load them on your Cricut Design Space.

- **Installation of Fonts into Design Space**

When you install the fonts, the next step is to load them into Design Space. Thus, in order to achieve this, you have to sign out of Design Space and re-sign in. After that, you'll also have to restart your PC. When this is done, you can check your Design Space account, where you'll see the new fonts in the display.

- **Changing/Replacing Blades**

Just like everything in life, nothing lasts forever, and Cricut blades are known to wear out. You will know it's time to change the blade when the cuts are no longer effective and smooth. That is the most obvious sign; however, there are a couple of others, including:

- Tearing vinyl or card
- Lifting of vinyl off the backing sheet
- Halfway cuts (wrong cut settings can also be responsible for this).

If you're convinced that your blades are no longer effective, you have to purchase new ones.

- **When the Mat Is No Longer Sticky**

The most proactive way of keeping your mat healthy over a long period is by cleaning it. However, if the mat is beyond redemption and there is no replacement yet, you should tape down your vinyl or card for it to stick. While tapping, you shouldn't tape the areas that are meant to be cut; just tape the sides. Most people use the medium tack painter tape because it allows a lot of room for this type of action, and it does not damage the cardstock.

- **Custom Settings for Cricut Machines**

There are 7 preset options on the dial for Explore Air 2, and they include:

i. Cardstock

ii. Paper

iii. Iron-on

iv. Vinyl

v. Poster board

vi. Light cardstock

vii. Bonded fabric

There is a custom option for materials that are not included in the cutting list, and you select it on the dial.

To do this, open Design Space, choose your project, and press 'Make it.' At this point, you'll see a prompt with a drop-down menu, where you'll be able to choose your material.

Likewise, you can also create a new custom material. There are resources on the Cricut website and all over the internet regarding the creation of custom material.

- **Use the Right Blade for the Right Material**

There are a number of crafters out there that use separate blades for cutting each material, e.g., let's say a crafter uses a dedicated blade to cut vinyl and another dedicated blade to cut cardstock. This practice is important because, from experience, different materials wear blades differently. Thus, it is easier for the blade to cut vinyl than to cut through the card.

If you have a particular blade for cutting vinyl materials, it means that the blade will be in prime condition. However, if you have a common blade that cuts everything, it'll easily go blunt and begin to find it difficult to cut through vinyl.

- **Whenever You Cut HTV, Always Mirror Your Image**

Make sure you mirror your design if you're cutting heat transfer vinyl with a Cricut machine. Whenever you hit the 'Make It' button, there is always an option for you to mirror your design. Thus, it is recommended that you use this option for each mat.

- **Make Sure Your HTV Is Properly Placed on the Cutting Mat**

If you intend to cut heat transfer vinyl, you have to place the shiny side of the vinyl down on the cutting mat. The whole idea is for the carrier sheet to be down and the dull side on top. This can be a little bit confusing at times, but you have to remember this: shiny side down always.

- **For Small and Intricate Designs, Use Weeding**

Weeding boxes are important, especially if you are cutting out a number of designs on a sheet of vinyl or just cutting out a little intricate design.

In Cricut Design Space, use the square tool to add a box around your design and join both elements together. Manipulate it into a rectangle by unlocking the shape at the bottom left corner.

When you do this, you'll realize that it is easier than concurrently weeding different designs on a sheet of vinyl. It is also easier than looking for your designs and using scissors to cut them out separately.

- **Always Set the Dial**

This is one of the best tips ever, but crafters tend to always forget to change the material settings on the machine. It is funny because before cutting, Cricut Design Space tells crafters the type of materials the dial is set to; however, it is not uncommon for them to overlook it and proceed to cut. Most times, crafters get overexcited after designing, that they only have cutting in their minds.

Mind you, setting your dial can save you the mistake of not cutting through your cardstock or cutting right through your cutting mat—the choice is yours.

- **Always Have a Constant Supply of Materials**

Just like it was said earlier, it is very hurtful to execute a project without the proper tools, e.g., I have been in the position of lacking the right pen for a project, being without the scoring stylus, not having a deep cut blade, etc. Furthermore, just imagine that you are about to start a project, and you suddenly realize that you don't have cardstock, HTV, or adhesive vinyl—it can be pretty sad.

Thus, you should always have a healthy supply of materials at all times, including: Cricut adhesive vinyl, a pad containing different colors of cardstock, and Cricut iron-on vinyl or a color bundle of Siser EasyWeed HTV.

If you have these items on hand, it is highly unlikely that you'll be caught out before or during the execution of any project.

Chapter 12: Tips for Solving Cricut Design Space Problems

Having some Cricut Design Space related problems?

Is your app crashing, freezing, loading slowly, or not even opening at all? You are unhappy about the situation because you want to start a new project, right?

These issues are widespread, and as such, we'll explore a few tips on actions to take when you're faced with Design Space problems.

Fixing Cricut Design Space Issues

When you put everything into consideration, it is safe to say that the Design Space software is very good.

 No system is perfect, and there's always room for improvement, but on the whole, the software works excellently for several projects. However, there are a couple of related issues that are predominant with the software, including; freezing, slow loading, crashing, and not opening at all. When you're faced with these issues, there are several things you can do to fix them:

- **Slow Internet Connection**

Without saying much, you must understand that a slow internet connection is one of the main causes of Design Space problems. Poor internet connection translates into problems for the software because it requires consistent download and upload speeds to function optimally.

Several websites only require good download speeds, e.g., YouTube; thus, users on these sites can do away with slow upload speeds. However, unlike those sites, Cricut Design Space requires good upload and download speeds to function optimally because users are constantly sending and receiving information as they progress with their designs.

Note: If you're using a modem, you're likely to have a more stable connection if you move closer to it.

Run a Speed Test

You can use a service like Ookla to run an internet speed test.

For Design Space to run optimally, Cricut specifies the following:

- Broadband connection

- Minimum 1–2 Mbps Upload

- Minimum 2–3 Mbps Download

After running the speed test, if the results are not good, and you are convinced that the connection is affecting your Design Space, you should wait until the connection improves or you call your service providers. There is also the option of switching to a new internet service provider with a proper internet connection.

- **Your Computer**

If you run a speed test and realize that your connection is fine, then your computer, mobile phone, or tablet might be the problem. Cricut has specific requirements for Design Space to function optimally. Below are some of the requirements:

Windows Computers

Your computer:

- Must have at least 4GB of ram

- Must be running on Windows 8 or later

- Must have Bluetooth connection or a free USB port

- Must have at least 50MB of free disk space

- Must have AMD processor or Intel Core series

Apple Computers

For Design Space to work optimally in your Mac computer, it must have the following:

- At least 50MB free space

- 4GB Ram

- Mac OS X 10.12 or a later version

- CPU of 1.83 GHz

Background Programs

If you're running too many background programs while using Design Space, it might also be a problem.

Some multi-tasking crafters are fond of engaging in different activities while designing on Design Space. For example, some simultaneously chat on Facebook, while downloading movies, watching videos on YouTube, and designing on Design Space. These activities will affect your app and make it malfunction badly; thus, it is important to shut down other projects and focus solely on Design Space.

While it is important to close other apps and shut down other activities, there are other things you should also do:

i.   Run a malware check

ii. If you're using windows, you should upgrade your drivers

iii. Clear your history and cache

iv. Defragment your hard drive

v.   Check your anti-virus software and update if needed

If you execute these tests, it might speed up the system or even solve all related problems.

- **Your Browser**

Your Design Space software might be having issues due to your system browser.

For you to access Design Space, Cricut recommends that you use the latest version of the browser you use. Be it Edge, Chrome, Firefox, or Mozilla; just make sure that it is up to date. If it refuses to work on a particular browser, open it in another browser to see if it works. Although the reasons are unknown, sometimes its work and even works perfectly.

- **Contact Cricut**

If you've tried all possible options and nothing works, you may have to call Cricut customer care to look into the issues you're faced with.

Cricut Cutting Problems and Solutions

Sometimes Cricut machines don't cut correctly and it is a common problem. For example, you spend hours buying materials and designing your project, but when the machine starts cutting, it destroys your material. This is something that has happened to a lot of people and will keep happening to those that have no idea about it in the future.

With that said, let's explore the possible solutions to the problem.

If you're faced with cutting problems, you have to check the following:

- Is your material sitting flat on your mat?

- Is your mat clean?

- Are you sure you're using the right mat for the material you're cutting?

- Is your blade clean?

- Is your blade dull?

- Are you using the right blade for the material you're cutting?

How to Change Settings

- Use the dial to change the cutting settings

- Use cardstock+ on the dial if you're using heavy cardstock

- If you're using the custom setting, turn the dial to custom. A list of materials will show up on your computer screen and you'll be able to choose the specific material you intend to cut

- Use Washi setting if you're using vinyl to cut your small or intricate design. To do this, you have to turn your dial to custom and look for Washi in the prompt that will pop up

Change the Font and Size

Sometimes, some images are just too intricate or too small to cut. Thus, if your image consists of intricate details or maybe you're using a distinctive font, then it might not cut properly until you get your size sorted.

- If possible, you will have to delete some part of your design

- Increase the size of your image

- Bolden the font

- Change/increase the font size if possible

- You can use a different program to thicken your font

Tips to Ensure You Get a Perfect Cut

- Make sure you run a test cut before you go ahead to cut your project.

- Ensure that you have the image 'set to cut' and not write or print.

- Make sure you mirror your image and turn over the paper if you are using a piece of loose glitter cardstock. When you do this, it helps the machine to cut without glitter getting stuck on the blade and in the housing.

- If you're using cardstock, flip over the textured side and make use of the smooth side always.

- If you successfully cut your project with tiny fonts, you can try reverse weeding to make it easier to transfer, especially if you're using vinyl.

The recommendations above are very helpful and will solve most of your cutting problems. However, if you've done everything and nothing seems to work, you should contact Cricut support. They are highly responsive and proactive. We know how most customer care service people behave at times, but with Cricut, you'll be dealing with a world-class team that is set up to help solve product-related issues.

On a final note, if you have explored all your options (including contacting Cricut support), and your cutting problem persists, it is possible that the brand or type of material you're using might be the problem. There are known cases where some brands of vinyl cardstock turned out to be bad for cutting.

Chapter 13: 9 Best Laptops for Cricut

People ask a lot of questions concerning the best laptops for Cricut machines because some laptops are just not made for certain purposes.

As we all know, Cricut produces die-cutting machines like the Cricut Explore Air, Air 2, and Cricut Maker that are used to cut felt, paper, fabric, vinyl, and other products for DIY projects and home use.

The machines have become a hit among women and it is used for scrapbooking many other homemade crafts.

As mentioned earlier, Cricut machines are cutting and plotting machines that get their directives from Cricut's very own Design Space browser-based software.

With the aid of the software, the machine cuts out online designs into real objects.

Though the software is browser-based, a reasonably powerful laptop is still a requirement for users to work efficiently with any hiccups.

Thus, this is a guide aimed at helping Design Space users choose the best laptop computer to use with the browser-based software.

With that said, below are nine best laptops for the Cricut Explore series:

Asus Vivobook F510UA

If you are not out for too much drama and just want to get the very best laptop for Cricut Explore Air and Air 2, then the Asus Vivobook F510UA is your guy.

With the 8th Generation Intel Core i5-8250U processor, it is one of the most up-to-date laptops that is capable of handling the Cricut Design Space software. The features of this particular laptop are awesome—it has a 15.6-inch Full HD screen tucked within a body of about 14-inch. Besides, there is a slim bezel surrounding the screen (about 0.3" thick), which gives the laptop an expensive look.

Ideally, Cricut machines are mostly used by women, and it is obvious that they prefer items that don't weigh too much. The Asus Vivobook F510UA is spot on because by weighing only 3.7 lbs. and it is considered a very light laptop and the lightest among the top nine best laptops for Cricut Explore Air and Air 2.

You can easily slide the laptop inside a backpack or laptop case because it is only 0.8" thick on the sides.

Although the Asus Vivobook F510UA is entirely plastic, it has a premium look, and Asus did extremely well to keep the price just under $500.

If you assess all areas concerning the best computer for Cricut Explore, then you'll realize that this laptop never disappoints.

The Asus Vivobook F510UA comes with: 1TB hard disk, 8GB RAM, latest Windows 10 operating system, future-proof-USB-C port, Screen-to-Body Ratio, and is of the rare traditional laptops that are not too expensive, as well as very easy to carry around.

This is the best laptop for Cricut Explore Air.

Dell Inspiron 15 5575

If you are one of those people that go after laptops from trusted brands, then it surely doesn't get better than Dell.

Though their earlier laptops were a bit pricey compared to other brands, the quality of their products has never been in doubt. These days, their laptops are mostly the same price as laptops from other brands such as HP and Lenovo, because of modern innovation and increased competition.

Dell Inspiron Series is their stand out brand and that is why they make sure it is routinely updated with the latest technologies in the industry.

The Dell Inspiron 15 5575 is built with AMD's latest Ryzen 5 2500U CPU, and it offers the same performance with the earlier mentioned Core-i5-8250U, and 20% more powerful than the older generation Intel Core i7-7500U.

Without mincing words, the Dell Inspiron 15 5575 is an extremely good laptop to use with Cricut Explore.

The bezels might not be as beautiful as the one on the Asus Vivobook F510UA; however, it is built with Full HD IPS display together with touch screen capability. With this, users have little use for the trackpad, and ideally won't even need to use an external mouse for designing on Cricut Design Space.

Together with the CPU, there is a dedicated AMD Radeon RX Vega 8 Graphics that boost the laptop's performance.

In terms of hardware, the laptop comes with an 8GB RAM, 1TB 5400RPM hard disk, as well as a 720p webcam.

In terms of weight, the Dell Inspiron 15 5575 weighs a little bit heavier than the Asus Vivobook F510UA. It weighs 4.48lbs and does not have the USB Type-C port.

In terms of connectivity, it comes with 2x USB 3.0, 2x USB 2.0, 1x HDMI and 1x headphone/microphone combo port.

The keyboard has a number pad and is backlit, and the keyboard panel has a small but durable touchpad with a smooth matte finish that extremely comfortable to touch.

For those that love to design, the Dell Inspiron 15 5575 design doesn't disappoint a bit. It comes in platinum silver color with a dark grey Dell logo etched on top, and the same color used on the screen panel.

Lenovo Ideapad 330S

Being a Chinese laptop, Lenovo is renowned for manufacturing laptops that offer value for money.

Lenovo's Ideapad series is meant for people in search of cheaper but powerful and durable laptops, mostly targeted towards young adults. In terms of power and design, the Lenovo's Ideapad series can't be left out because it comes with the right mix.

The Lenovo Ideapad 330S is no exception because it is built with minimal design and the top is mostly blank, except for the Lenovo logo that appears towards the left corner of the lid.

When the lid is open, you'll see the Lenovo branding at the left side of the screen bezel, dipped in black with a glossy finish on the logo. When you study Lenovo's branding, you'll realize that the company puts product viability and durability ahead of branding.

Lenovo Ideapad 330S is not only good looking, but it is also the most powerful laptop in this list because it comes with Intel Core i7-8550U CPU along with Intel's own UHD 620 Graphics that speeds up graphical elements in the Cricut Design Space application.

Lenovo Ideapad 330S comes with a 4GB RAM; however, on its page on Amazon, it costs an extra $60 to upgrade it to 8GB RAM.

Just like the Dell Inspiron 15 5575, the Lenovo Ideapad 330S has a full-size keyboard that contains a number pad; the only difference is that the spacing between the keys is smaller.

Also, the touchpad is larger than the one on the Dell Inspiron 15 5575, just that the keyboard backlighting is absent.

In terms of connectivity, Lenovo Ideapad 330S has 2x USB 3.0, 1x USB-C, 1xHDMI, and 1x headphone/microphone combo jack.

Sadly, the deal breaker is that it comes with a 1366x768 screen resolution, as opposed to a 1920x1080 Full HD screen.

Asus Vivobook S410UN

If you want a very tiny laptop, then the Asus Vivobook S410UN is the perfect machine for you.

Just like the Asus Vivobook F510UA, it is a great combination of power and style because it comes with a powerful Intel Core i7-8550U process combined with Nvidia MX 150 GPU.

The Asus Vivobook S410UN has an 8GB DDR4 RAM, along with a 256GB SSD storage.

On the surface level, 256GB storage seems very small compared to the 1TB present in other laptops; however, SSD storage is five to ten times faster than a regular hard disk and will help to speed up your work.

It is perfect for people that use their Cricut Explore Air for commercial purposes, where every second count.

In terms of design, the Asus Vivobook S410UN looks much like the earlier mentioned Vivobook S510UA, only that it has a smaller frame.

It has a 14-inch screen with Full HD resolution, and the screen display is very sharp, compared to Full HD display on 15.6" displays.

Due to the size of the screen, the laptop's width is exactly 13.2-inch, and this, in turn, reduces the laptop's weight to exactly 3.2 lbs.

On the sides, the Asus Vivobook S410UN is only 0.7" thick, with a 77% screen-to-body ratio, which is perfect for the size.

Also, the Asus Vivobook S410UN comes with a backlit keyboard and a fingerprint sensor built within the trackpad.

Users can log into the laptop without a password by using the fingerprint sensor and the Windows Hello feature.

In terms of connectivity, the laptop comes with 1xUSB 3.1 Type-C, 1x USB 3.0, 2xUSB 2.0, Bluetooth 4.2 Dual-Band Wi-Fi, 42WH Battery, and 1xHDMI.

This is a very small laptop that you can carry around in your backpack without knowing or feeling that you're even carrying anything.

Acer Predator Helios 300

The Acer Predator Helios 300 does not only possess high-end performance, but it also comes with specific features that make it compatible with the Cricut Explore Air.

Several features make the laptop stand out and in terms of design, you'll surely love it.

It is specifically built for users that seek sleek, high end, and high-speed performance laptops at a reasonable price.

It has a display size of 15.6-inch, 1.05-inch chassis, and a 144Hz screen. The 144Hz indicates high end visual and graphic facility with ultimate gaming speed.

The Acer Predator Helios 300 possesses GTX 1060 6GB GPU and its CPU, Intel 6-Core i7-8750H is extremely powerful. In terms of storage, it comes with 16GB DDR4 RAM and 256GB PCIe NVMe SSD. Thus, users will love its high-end performance and functions because the storage enhances its speed and functionality.

It is very hard to find a portable, high-end performance laptop, and the Acer Predator Helios 300 is no exception. It weighs about 5.5lbs (2.5kg), meaning it's not something that can be moved easily around.

Another con about this product is the fact that it approximately works for about 5 hours on standard usage. Thus, if you're someone that is looking for a system that can run over long periods, then this isn't suitable for you.

However, if you consider the overall performance of this laptop, along with its compatibility with Cricut Explore Air, then you will never get it wrong.

Acer Aspire 7

A high-end performance laptop like the Acer Aspire 7 hardly disappoints, and it is one laptop that is highly compatible with Cricut Explore Air.

With this laptop, you can create awesome designs because it comes with the 4.1 GHz Intel Core i7 coupled with NVIDIA GeForce GTX1050Ti 4GB, 8GB DDR4, which empowers the system to run heavy software. With its 16GB RAM, it is understandable why it is such a compatible system for Cricut machines.

The Acer Aspire 7 comes with 128GB SSD plus 1TB HDD storage, making it easy for users to multitask. And with the SSD, it is about 5-10x faster than regular laptops with hard disks.

With the dual-microphone system that enhances call quality and the HD fit-in cameras, users will be able to enjoy high-quality video calls. Also, its advanced 2x2 MIMO wireless technology processes data twice the speed of traditional laptops.

It comes with USB 3.1 Type C Gen 1 standard USB port with a speed of 5Gbps, plus it also has a fingerprint sensor.

In terms of portability, the Acer Aspire 7 weighs approximately 5.1 lbs. (2.2kg), a little bit too heavy to move around with.

The laptop has a beautiful keyboard with smooth and soft-touch features. It also has a Full HD display of 15.6-inches.

It is a pocket-friendly laptop with a stunning design, excellent memory, and fast speed. With the Acer Aspire 7, you can take your crafting to the next level.

Asus ZenBook 13

Purchasing a laptop involves a cost that cannot be overlooked. Even more, if you want the latest version at an affordable price. The Asus ZenBook 13 is a laptop for all budgets. With a 13.3-inch. IPS display offers smaller bezels than the previous versions at the top and corners, which makes it incredible. Its CPU under the cowl is Intel Core i5-8265U. It does not have GPU quality, which makes it the wrong model for you if you are looking for it. This laptop model offers a great storage facility for multitasking.

When it comes to portability, Asus Zenbook 13 is very light, weighing only 2.5 lbs. (1.1 kg), which is very convenient to carry. The battery life goes for up to 9 hours with multitasking, making it compatible with Cricut Explore Air.

Specifications

With a screen size of 13.3 inches, weighing 2.5 lbs., a storage capacity of 512 GB SSD, a RAM of 8GB DDR3, an Intel Core i5-8265U processor, a graphics card Intel HD Graphics 620, and a Windows 10 Home as operating system, this laptop is of great value for its price. Overall, a very good laptop to purchase. Unfortunately, it lacks GPU quality, which would have been good to include.

Asus VivoBook S

Asus VivoBook S is the most suitable and appropriate laptop for Cricut Explore Air. This laptop is for everyday users, giving them the tool they need to work properly, fulfilling their requirements.

Very well designed, this laptop is an eye-catcher with its bright colors. With a 14 inches display and few numbers of bezels with two slides, it is a very attractive laptop. Though not of high-end performance, its specifications remain palatable, namely being of its 8th generation Intel Core i7-8550U Central Processing Unit (QUAD-CORE PROCESSOR), its 14 inches Full HD wide-view nano edge display (1920×1080). Finally, its storage capacity of 256GB SSD, 8GB DDR4 RAM, and GeForce GTX MX 150 are features that cannot be overlooked.

Acer Aspire E 15

The Acer Aspire E 15 is a wise choice for people that recently purchased the Cricut Explore Air 2 and are not willing to spend another huge amount on a brand new laptop.

When compared to other laptops on the list, the Acer Aspire E 15 isn't as powerful; however, it is still a powerful machine for the Cricut Design Space application.

In terms of design, the Acer Aspire E 15 doesn't look too good, and there's nothing fancy to say about it in that department.

The laptop is built entirely out of plastic, but it has a functional design with a brushed metal finish in the top lid and keyboard panel.

The Acer Aspire E 15 comes with Intel Core i3-8130U process with 6GB RAM, 1TB HDD, and an 8X DVD Drive.

With a price of around $350, it still comes with a Full HD display with pre-installed Windows 10 OS, as well as LED backlighting.

It comes with USB 3.0 port and USB 3.1 Type-C port and because it mostly contains low power consuming hardware, the Acer Aspire E 15 has a battery life of over 10 hours, which remains the highest in the list of best laptops for Cricut Explore Air.

When you consider the price, it is an excellent piece of hardware; however, you should only purchase this laptop if you're working with a very tight budget.

Otherwise, the best laptop for Cricut Air remains the Asus Vivobook F510UA.

Chapter 14: 4 Best Software to Use with Cricut and Create Amazing Design Templates

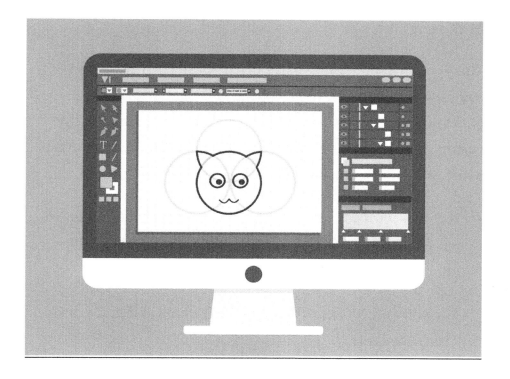

For craft enthusiasts and people that love the Cricut die-cutting system, it is no longer news that digital die-cutting units are extremely restrictive.

They mostly allow users to cut a small number of fonts and they are not cheap at all.

Thankfully, there are a few programs out there that have managed to open Cricut to enable them to cut designs, TrueType fonts created by users, and many more.

Below is a list of the best third-party software to use with Cricut.

Make the Cut

This is an awesome third-party Cricut Design software that comes with simple but highly effective design features, e.g., it packs quick lattice tools, and it can convert raster images into vectors for cutting. The program has been around for some time. Some of the most outstanding features of the tool include:

- It comes with advanced editing tools, and it is quite easy to use (even for a newbie) because the user interface is effortless to learn.

- The software works with many file formats and it also uses TrueType fonts.

- The software comes with a pixel trace tool that allows users to take and convert raster graphics into vector paths for cutting.

- For those that are interested, Make The Cut works with Gazelle, Craft ROBO, Wishblade, and Silhouette.

- Some other features include the fact that users can import the following: WPC, GSD, PS, AI9, EPS, OTF, TTF, SCUT, or PDF files and can also export shapes in SVG, PDF, Ai, EPS, PNG, and JPG formats.

Make The Cut is a user-friendly and flexible Cricut related software that adds more utility to the digital die-cutting machine that is normally limited in terms of usage and application.

Sure Cuts A Lot

The Sure Cuts A Lot software gives users complete control of their designs without the restrictions of cartridges featured in Cricut DesignStudio.

Users must install a firmware update to their Cricut die-cutting machine; however, they can do this for free by downloading the trial version of DesignStudio. It is a very easy task to perform.

Some of the features of the Sure Cuts A Lot software include:

- It allows users to use the OpenType and TrueType fonts.

- It is the one and only Cricut Design tool available that comes with freestyle drawing tools.

- It allows users to create personal designs with basic drawing and editing tools.

- The program works with Silhouette, Craft ROBO, and Wishblade die-cutting machines.

- It is specifically designed to open up all of Cricut's cutting features and abilities.

- It allows users to edit the individual nodes that make up the path.

- It comes with an auto trace feature that converts raster graphics into vector images.

- The programs has about 200 built-in shapes and other exciting features.

- It allows users to import different file-formats including: PDF, SVG, AI, EPS, and WPC. The pro version allows users to import DXF and PLT.

- It allows users to select styles including Blackout and Shadow, to change the looks of shapes and letters easily with just a few clicks of the mouse.

- It allows users to use advanced features such as layers, grouping, as well as the weld tool, in order to make the most out of their designs.

To download and get the complete set of features of Sure Cuts A Lot, you can check their website. The Sure Cuts A Lot program doesn't come with fonts, it only allows users to make use of the fonts that are already on their computers.

Getting more fonts to your computer isn't a big deal because there are thousands of fonts out there. Besides, you don't have to buy any special cartridges to get more fonts to your system.

Cricut DesignStudio

Cricut DesignStudio, a product of ProvoCraft is a program that allows users to connect Cricut to a personal computer so that they can do much more with Cricut fonts and shapes.

For those that don't know, Provo Craft is the same company that manufactures Cricut die-cutting machines. With the aid of various tools, this Cricut software allows users to adjust fonts and shapes.

Some of the best features of the software include:

- Users will be able to weld, flip, and rotate easily.

- Users have the option of previewing and creating designs with different images from the Cricut library.

- Users will have to purchase a cartridge to cut.

- The software comes with a high level of customization to the Cricut library, and the extra features are very helpful.

- People that use this software are still limited to the same shapes and fonts from the cartridges they own, but bearing in mind the tools that are packed in the program, that is not an issue.

The program remains a very good option to use alongside your Cricut, and you'll be able to get the best out of its features. To know more about the software, go to their official website.

Inkscape

Inkspace is an open-source graphics editor for Windows and other operating systems. It is a professional program that costs absolutely nothing.

Users can use the program along with Cricut to create and edit vector graphics such as illustrations, diagrams, line arts, logos, elaborate paintings, and much more.

Below are some of the features that come with the software:

- It can be used to render primitive text and vector shapes.

- It supports embedding and optional tracing of raster graphics.

- The objects can be filled with solid colors, patterns, radial, linear color gradients, and others; their borders can be stroked with adjustable transparency.

- The program can be used to create vector graphics from multiple raster sources and pictures.

- Shapes created can be manipulated easily with different transformations that include: moving, rotating, scaling, and skewing.

There are many more features present in this powerful software, and the easiest way to get acquainted with them all is to visit Inkscape's official website.

In order to maximize the use of your Cricut machine, you should consider using these awesome software applications that are compatible with Windows systems.

For the best experience possible, you should pair them up with some 2D digital pixel art tools or with some photo editors.

Depending on what you choose to do, you will easily take control of your creativity and use Cricut Design Space the way you've always dreamt of.

Chapter 15: How to Make a Business with Your Cricut Machine

The creativity of your designs and the skill you will develop can allow you to create and start your own business if you wish. For enthusiastic novices, many questions would be faced, such as:

1) Where Do I Start?

Like any start-up business, initial questions need to be addressed to overcome possible difficulties. For example, addressing issues like defining my clientele, the products that might be of interest, where to find them, and how to make a profit margin of my sales are important to tackle from the start. In other words, you will need a good and well-defined business strategy to start with.

2) Choosing My Clientele

You can target two avenues to sell your products: either by looking at how you can approach the market locally or online. It is advisable to concentrate efforts on one approach to start with as your target is to generate profits as soon as possible. Never forget that your goal is to grow benefits and reinvest it so that your business expands. The quicker you increase your sales, the more likely you will reinvest in new tools or new products, making, in turn, a stronger financial turnover. Understanding your marketing strategy is the key to your success.

3) Approaching Local Markets

You can explore selling your products from 'business to business.' In this configuration, the volume of sales is of importance as the larger the production, the lower the production cost per item is. This is the most challenging balance to reach for a new Cricut based business. The advantage of obtaining contractual work means you can negotiate to buy a large quantity from vendors. However, such 'golden' opportunities are hard to find since such contracts are opened to competition. Yet, as a new start-up business, you can present your products specifically tailored for business customers. A custom work approach offers positive aspects as businesses always look for originality and good products. By creating such a relationship, your business is likely to become a point of reference for future other contacts, hence launching many opportunities for upselling. However, it is important to bear in mind that finding such a niche is hard as competition is very stiff!

Another approach to consider for selling your products is from 'business to customer.' In this model, though the volume of sales remains important, your objective is to present your products to retail customers willing to buy them. Creativity, imagination will be the keys to your success, as well as what type of media and medium you want to work in (e.g., T-shirts, mugs). Equally important is a retail space you will need to choose to offer your items. Experiencing different locations and products is all part of the efforts of a new start-up business. Also, a custom work approach for local customers will present advantages since the start-up costs are the lowest of all the different strategies described so far. However, as a new business in the field, starting can be difficult. Word of mouth can be your first step, as well as producing good products at an affordable price.

4) Selling Online

If you are adept at higher technical knowledge, then you can generate great benefits by providing either quality custom work, bulk offering, or information network. It is advisable to concentrate your efforts on one approach to start with. If you choose, for example, a custom work approach, you increase the chances to find potential customers looking for your products as they turn to a search engine like Google to find what they are looking for. Websites like Amazon Handmade or Etsy provide a good platform to allow to sell custom design services. Equally efficient is the launch of your site. This strategy is worth looking at. Selling online presents advantages such as low start-up costs and access to the global market with millions of potential customers. Furthermore, online custom prices tend to be lower than those on the local market. However, access to the global market means that competition is stiff, pushing products to be competitively priced. Selling online requires certain knowledge in logistics as far as shipping and packing your products are concerned, a cost factor that needs to be taken into consideration in your pricing.

Suppose the approach of bulk offering or volume sales is the one that you prefer. In that case, the advantages are similar to those discussed under 'approaching local markets,' namely reducing the cost per unit produced. Amazon and eBay have become the largest platforms. On the other hand, if an online retail business approach is more what you may be inclined to do, then this approach will give you the ability to determine the demand for the designs you offer and plan the production accordingly. But selling online means challenging the existing competition!

Finally, if you prefer to sell your products online through information networks, then you become an authority in the field, creating the opportunity to generate profit with your Cricut designs. By offering blogs on technical know-how or inspiration work, you become selective on the posts you want to take on.

Starting a new business requires foremost a business strategy, the foundation for your future success. Asking yourself who your potential customers would be, what kind of products you can sell them, and how are the first steps of a future startup business.

Chapter 16: How to Make Money with Your Cricut Machine

In terms of making money from the comfort of your home, you easily achieve that with a Cricut machine. However, you have to bear in mind that there are a number of competitors out there, thus, you have to put in extra effort in order to stand a chance to succeed.

For you to become successful in the Cricut world of crafts, you have to keep the following in mind:

1. Dare to Be Different

You have to be yourself, unleash your quirkiness and creativity.

Those that have been in the Cricut world of crafts for some time know all about the knockout name tiles. They became a hit and in no time, everyone was producing and selling them.

In the crafting world, that is the norm. Thus, you could be among the earliest people to jump on a trend to ride the wave until the next hot seller surfaces. Mind you, that strategy of selling Cricut crafts can become costly and tiresome if you are not careful.

The basic idea here is to add your flair and personal style, and not to completely re-invent the wheel. For example, let's say you come across two name tiles on Etsy, one looks exactly like the other 200+ on sale on the site, while the second one has a few more tweaks and spins on it. The seller of the second product will possibly charge more and accrue a higher profit because his/her product is unique and stands out from the rest.

When you design your products, don't be afraid to tweak your fonts, because even the simplest of tweaks and creativity can make your product stand out from the rest.

Remember this; if you create a product that looks exactly like others, you are only putting yourself in a 'price war,' where no one usually wins.

2. Keep It Narrow

A lot of crafters out there believe that creating and selling everything under the sun translates into more patronage and more money, but that isn't how it works. On the contrary, it might only result in a huge stock of unsold products, more burn out, and heavy cost. Rather than producing materials here and there, you should focus on being the best in your area of craftiness, so that when people need specific products in your area, they'll come to you.

It can be very tempting to want to spread your tentacles because it might seem like the more you produce, the more options you'll provide for your clients, but that might be counterproductive.

Take out time to think about your area of strength and focus your energy on making products that you'd be known for. It is better to be known as an expert in a particular product than to be renowned for someone that produces a high number of inferior products.

Thus, you should keep it narrow and grow to become the very best in your area of craft.

3. Be Consistent

If you intend to become successful, you have to consistently work on your Cricut craft business. Some people work once a week or thereabout because they sell as a hobby; however, if you intend to make in-road in your business, you have to work every day.

If you have other engagements and can't work every day, then you should create a weekly schedule and stick to it. If you shun your business for weeks and months at a time, then you will not go anywhere with it.

Apart from consistency in work and production, you also have to be consistent with your product quality and pricing. When your customers are convinced about your products, they will easily recommend you to their friends, family, business partners, and many others.

In business, there are ups and downs, thus, you shouldn't reduce your work rate because things are not going as planned. Success doesn't come easy, but one of the surest ways of being and maintaining success is by consistently doing the things you love.

4. Be Tenacious

It is not easy to run a business because it involves a lot of hard work, sweat, and even heartbreaks. Thus, you have to bear in mind that there will be days when you will feel like throwing in the towel. There will be days when nothing go as planned. There will also be days when customers will tick you off. You will feel like a drowning boat because you're working hard but nothing is working out.

However, you have to look at the bigger picture, because the crafting business is not a get rich quick scheme. Remember, quitters never win, so quitting isn't an option. Keep doing the things you love, and keep improving. Successful people never give up. They suffer many setbacks but they don't stop.

Thus, for you to be successful in your craft, you have to be tenacious and resilient. Be willing to maneuver your way through tough times, and do not forget to pick up lessons.

5. Learn Everyday

Be willing to learn from people that have been successful in the business. You don't necessarily have to unravel everything by yourself, because whatever it is you are doing, others have already done it in the past.

Whether you intend to learn how to build a successful Facebook group or how to go up the Etsy ranks, remember that people have already done all that in the past, and are giving out tricks and tips they know.

Make it a tradition to learn something new about your business every day because, at the beginning of your business, you will have to do more marketing than crafting.

When you wake up in the morning, browse through the internet, gather materials, and read in your spare time, because the more you learn, the better your chances of being successful. They say knowledge is power, and for you to become successful as a craftsman/woman, you have to constantly seek new knowledge in the form of tips, tricks, software upgrades, marketing, design ideas, tools, accessories, and many others.

All I am saying is that you should learn without ceasing.

6. Quality Control

If you intend to grow your brand, you must prioritize the selling of high-quality products. Your motto should quality over everything.

For you to easily succeed, people should know you as someone that sells top quality products, because quality wins over quantity every day of the week.

You don't want to be known as someone that produces poor quality items because when the word spreads (and it surely will), your business will pack up.

If you focus your attention and efforts on the production of high-quality materials, you will be able to withstand competition, no matter how stiff it is.

Conclusion

Cricut machines are awesome gadgets to own because they do not only boost creativity and productivity; they can also be used to create crafts for business. With Design Space, crafters can create almost anything and even customize their products to bear their imprints.

All over the world, people use these machines to make gift items, T-shirts, interior décor, and many other crafts; to beautify their homes, share with friends and family during holidays, sell, etc.

There are two types of Cricut machines; the Cricut Explore and the Cricut Maker. Both machines are highly efficient in their rights, and experts in the crafting world make use of them to create a plethora of items, either as a hobby or for business.

Both machines are similar in many ways, i.e., the Cricut Maker and the Explore Air 2, but the Cricut Maker is somewhat of a more advanced machine because it comes with some advanced features, as compared to the Explore Air 2.

One distinct feature about the Maker that sets it apart from the Explore Air is the fact that it can cut thicker materials. With the Maker, the possibilities are limitless and crafters can embark on projects that were never possible with Cricut machines before the release of the Maker.

Another feature that puts the Cricut Maker machine ahead of the Explore Air 2 is the 'Adaptive Tool System.' With this tool, the Cricut Maker has been empowered in such a way that it will remain relevant for many years to come because it will be compatible with new blades and other accessories that Cricut will release in the foreseeable future.

Although both machines have several dissimilarities, there are also areas where they completely inseparable. Take, for example, the designing of projects in Cricut Design Space.

Cricut Design Space is the software where all the magnificent designs are made before they are sent to be cut. It is one of the most important aspects in the creation of crafts in the Cricut setup. However, when it comes to Cricut Maker and the Explore Air 2, there is nothing to separate them in this regard, because both machines use the same software for project design.

As a crafter, without proper knowledge of Design Space, you're not only going to cut out poor products, you will also make little or no in-road in your quest to find success.

Understanding Design Space is important because it empowers crafters with enormous tools and materials to create generalized and custom products. It is an extremely powerful tool that just cannot be overlooked by anyone who intends to follow this path.

Thus, the understanding of Design Space is a must for people that intend to make a business out of Cricut machines or even utilize it as a hobby. With the software, crafters can create their designs from scratch or use already-made designs on the Cricut platform. Those that have an active subscription on Cricut Access have access to thousands of images, projects, and fonts. They can cut out their products using these images or projects, and they can also edit them to suit their style and taste before cutting.

Cricut Design Space comes with some exciting tools and features that can make crafting easy and straightforward. These tools are not so hard to use; thus, in order to get conversant with them, you need to do some research and consistently apply the knowledge you gain from your research and reading. Expert crafters know all about the important tools in Cricut Design Space, as well as the role they play in the design of projects. Some of these tools include: the slice tool, weld tool, contour tool, attach tool, flatten tool, etc.

Cricut machines do not function separately—when you purchase them, they come with accessories and tools that are required for them to function. Minus the tools and accessories that come in the pack, there are also others that can be purchased separately in order to boost the machine's functionality and output. In this book, we have discussed the basic accessories and tools that are needed for crafters to use along with their machines for optimum functionality and ease of design and production.

In terms of the Cricut Design Space software and app, some tips and tricks aid the process of project design and production. The software is easy and straightforward to learn and design on, but like every other application and software, it still has some related issues and problems.

When problems arise, solutions are naturally proffered, and in terms of Cricut Design Space, there are several ways to address app-related issues to improve user experience and functionality. This book covers several solutions to the issues related to the Design Space app and software.

The Cricut Design Space software is now an app; thus, some laptop computers are perfectly suited for the purpose. These laptops are suitable for several reasons, including: speed, space, design, etc. In summary, the best five are: Asus Vivobook F510UA, Dell Inspiron 15 5575, Lenovo Ideapad 330S, Asus Vivobook S410UN, and the Acer Aspire E 15.

Everything on earth needs maintenance, including Cricut machines. These machines are constantly cutting out materials of different textures, shapes, quantity, etc. Thus, they need routine maintenance in order to boost their productivity levels and increase their life span.

The routine maintenance of these machines does not require a lot, and as a matter of fact, the hardware needs cleaning after cutting out materials. Thus, non-alcoholic baby wipes are highly recommended for cleaning material residue on the machines. The cutting mat is another item that needs maintenance from time to time because excessive usage without proper care reduces its stickiness.

In terms of projects, there are so many items that can be designed and cut out from Cricut machines.

Also, these items can be sold in the crafts market for profit. Although some people use the machines for recreational purposes, there are even a higher number of people who use it for commercial purposes.

Commercial users of Cricut machines design and cut out items to sell for profit and the machines have proven to be a blast.

One of the reasons why people can sell items made from Cricut machines is because they have the option of creating custom and unique products that cannot be found anywhere else.

Cricut machines are awesome tools that should be on everybody's radar, especially people that love crafts.